Romancing the 50s

Romancing the 50s

Nargis, RK, Radio, and a Wistful Indian

Harjap Singh Aujla

THE BROWSER

Title: Romancing the 50s
Nargis, RK, Radio, and a Wistful Indian
Author: Harjap Singh Aujla

ISBN: 978-93-92210-80-8

Edition: I

Published by:
JGS Enterprises Pvt Ltd
Imprint: The Browser

Publisher's Address:
SCO 14-15, Sector 8-C, Chandigarh 160009
Website: www.thebrowser.org
Email: service@thebrowser.org

Editing, Layout and Cover Design by 99 beagles
www.99beagles.com

THE BROWSER
Publishers & Booksellers

Contents

MUSINGS

Author's Note

My childhood was thoroughly influenced by my well-educated parents. I was initiated into listening to radio broadcasts by my mother, who hooked me to listening to radio as a hobby, thus keeping me occupied for hours. I tuned in to distant stations, available on short-wave and medium-wave, at night. This hobby developed into a full-scale obsession, which transformed me into an admirer of music of all kinds, including classical, semi-classical, folk, country, jazz, and film music, both Indian and Western. The subject of radio and music is a frequent topic in this book.

My scholarly father, Late Sardar Sochet Singh, often took me along to the cinema hall in my early years to watch what later became some of the best movies of the 1950s. It inculcated a love for good and well-meaning cinema. I was initiated into watching movies when I was merely five years old. The first four films that I watched were in 1949—*Barsaat, Mahal, Andaz,* and *Bari Behen.* All proved to be great musicals and commercially hit movies. My father was a member of the Constituent Assembly of India, and we were mostly in New Delhi during those days, which was soon after the independence of India. At that age, I could not recapitulate the storyline of any of these films, but to my amazement, I could pick up the tunes and lyrics of most of the songs of these vintage beauties. In particular, I remembered the first few words of all the songs of the Nargis-Raj Kapoor starrer *Barsaat (1949)*. I tried to watch most of their movies in later years. A section of this book is dedicated to the exceptional merits of Nargis and Raj Kapoor. This includes the special contribution of the duo of music directors Shanker and Jaikishan, along with lyricists Hasrat Jaipuri and Shailendra.

As years passed, my love for films increased, and I started listening to the Hindi (commercial service) of Radio Ceylon on short-wave. I subsequently watched the films *Awaara* (1951), *Bewafa* (1952), *Aah* (1953), *Shree 420* (1955), and *Chori Chori* (1956). All these movies had a common factor—the leading pair of Nargis and Raj Kapoor and the enchanting music of Shanker and Jaikishan.

I was also an ardent admirer of the music of Pandit Amar Nath, Anil Biswas, Pandit Husan Lal, Bhagat Ram, C. Ramchandra, Sajjad Hussain, Shyam Sunder, Jaidev, Naushad Ali, Madan Mohan, Vinod, and Sachin Dev Burman. They were all exceptional. Yet, except for *Bewafa, Ashiana,* and just a few other movies, all the Nargis-Raj Kapoor movies mentioned above had the music of Shanker and Jaikishan. I developed some sort of infatuation towards the music of the duo, too. The lyrics of these songs were given by two young men, Hasrat Jaipuri and Shailendra. Without understanding the lyrics, I liked their words too because those words perfectly matched the grammar of the raga in which each song was composed.

I watched all the films produced in R. K. Studios, starring Nargis and Raj Kapoor, at least three times, and had the appetite for watching each of them more often. My command of Hindi was, at best, poor, but I enjoyed Raj Kapoor's dialogues in the easy-to-understand Hindustani language as well as the simple but elegant diction of Nargis' Urdu. I watched their films so many times that both became *de facto* members of my make-believe family. Watching videos of their movies and songs became a part of my daily routine. I knew that Raj Kapoor was married. But after repeatedly watching the unique equation between the duo on the film screen, I could not contemplate the existence of Raj Kapoor's angelic better half, Krishna Kapoor, who was a very quiet and decent lady. After becoming an author, it occurred to me to put into writing my views and analyses of the Nargis and Raj Kapoor duo, especially after watching their films repeatedly.

I had two close friends in the film industry. Both were music directors of lesser fame than the ones mentioned above. One was S. Mohinder, an extremely hardworking gentleman who was always driven by the urge to do better. The other was Sardul Singh Kwatra, a genius capable of generating excellent results with much less labour. Both gave me an insight into their own experiences with the most brilliant pair of actors in the film industry.

The book also contains brief anecdotes from my life and career as an engineer in the USA and India—I hope the readers will find them interesting. Radios are my favourite electronic gadgets, and I have collected several of them. I listen to them regularly. I have had the pleasure of seeing some exotic-looking radios in the museums. There is a story on the transformation of radios from being bulky to becoming beautifully shaped floor-mounted wooden cabinet mono radios made from valves and tubes along with massive speakers, and then to stereo sound-producing valve radios and transistorised and miniaturised radios of the modern era. One chapter deals with my childhood favourite—Radio Ceylon, now called Sri Lanka Broadcasting Corporation, based in Colombo, the capital of Sri Lanka.

There are stories about some Indians in America who covered themselves with glory by their spirit of social service to the neighbourhoods they dwelt in. There is also a story about how some highly intelligent and politically oriented Indians, in their own way, are influencing the results of American elections in some of the closely contested electoral districts.

There is also a write-up on the transition and shifting of the Punjabi cinema industry from the studios in Punjab's capital, Lahore, to the tinsel town of Bombay (now Mumbai), to eventually, settling down in Mohali (Punjab). There is another story about a nine-decade-old gramophone that we own, which is still in working order!

After going to the USA, I came to know that most common Americans knew only about two band radios—AM/FM (Amplitude Modulation and Frequency Modulation)—and they were ignorant about the existence of inter-continental short-wave broadcasting and the world's most popular and most regularly heard radio station, the BBC of London. There is another story on the use of short-wave radio stations as a weapon of the Cold War between the USA and its allies on one side and the erstwhile Soviet Union and its allies on the other side. One story is about the collapse of the Twin Towers of the World Trade Center in Downtown Manhattan in New York City and its aftermath.

In the game of cricket, one phrase is commonly used—catches win matches. I have tried to practically prove it correct while managing the Punjab Engineering College Cricket team. One story explains the red-tapism in Indian *Babushahi*, how it has crippled the work culture for decades, and how we got over it in one chronically delayed case.

Nowadays, we take the Internet and its offshoots for granted. I have dwelt on the dull and dreary pre-Internet phase in the USA and the world. You will be surprised to know that in an advanced country like America, the Indian *jugad* can solve some of the ticklish engineering problems.

With a high degree of success, I have used Indian tours of the engineering students from the Punjab Engineering College, Chandigarh, to teach them a course included in their syllabus. A chapter in this book deals with it.

The readers will find some strange but very interesting material in this book, which will link them to the past.

Chandigarh
January 2024

Harjap Singh Aujla
harjapaujla@gmail.com

Part-I

CINEMA

Nargis and Raj Kapoor

I am a die-hard admirer of the twentieth-century Indian film industry's leading actor pair, Nargis and Raj Kapoor. Listening to their dialogues and songs is a part of my everyday routine. My way of remembering them consists of watching their evergreen films and listening to songs that have been romantically picturised as duets, solos, and others. Whenever I feel like it, I watch their films produced under the R. K. and other banners.

The song that I remember the most and listen to at least once a week is the very popular *Raja Ki Aayegi Baraat* from the once-flopped film *Aah* (1953). Its *alaap* in the sweet silken voice of India's finest playback singer, Lata Mangeshkar, touches my heart. Lata Mangeshkar was guided under the music direction of Shanker and Jaikishan. It is a melody par excellence. I am taking the liberty to rate it as one of the best songs of the Indian film industry of the twentieth century. Once, another music director, S. Mohinder, told me that on an unscheduled visit, Raj Kapoor heard a tune composed by him in his (S. Mohinder's) office and requested permission to use it in one of his films.

S. Mohinder unhesitatingly accepted the suggestion, but Shanker and Jaikishan, powered by their orchestra, made it better than the original tune. The song was *Raja Ki Aayegi Baraat*. The other songs that I enjoy include *Dam Bhar Jo Udhar (Awaara,* 1951*)*, rendered by Lata Mangeshkar and Mukesh, and *Yeh Shaam Ki Tanhaiyan* and *Jo Main Jaanti Unke Liye*, both from the film *Aah* (1953). Another great song that has been picturised on Nargis is *Rasik Balma* from *Chori Chori* (1956). This film was full of sweet melodies. Yet another sweet song is *Man Bhavan Ke Ghar Jaye*. *Yeh Raat Bheegi Bheegi* from the same film is also extremely melodious and soulful—with the Manna Dey and Lata Mangeshkar duet. All the other songs are in the evergreen voice of the Bharat Ratna recipient Lata Mangeshkar, who unfortunately died due to Covid-19 and its aftereffects in May 2022. Lata Mangeshkar, indeed, played a huge role in the superstardom of both Nargis and Raj Kapoor.

Several authors have written about Nargis and Raj Kapoor. All of them acquired in-depth knowledge about the film industry's most successful pair. As written above, I have seen their films several times and the inferences that I could draw find a place in this chapter. But before I move on to the reasons for Nargis-Raj Kapoor's success, I must note that no other duo will ever be like theirs. I also dare say that India will never be a poor nation as long as, among other precious assets, the Nargis-Raj Kapoor films stay our national asset.

One of the things that worked for the Nargis-Raj Kapoor duo dawned on me when I was looking at the pictures of Jaddan Bai, Nargis' illustrious mother. From the looks of it, she was an extremely elegant, sweet, pleasant, attractive, and full-of-charm lady from North India who, under a well-thought plan, meticulously trained her daughter to become a great actor and an even better broad-minded human being. Eventually, Nargis turned out to be a perfect cinema star, a worthy wife to the gentle and suave actor-husband Sunil Dutt, and a loving and caring mother to a son and two daughters. She could have done a lot more for her family had she had a longer and healthier life. Overall, in her professional modernity and adaptability, she was way ahead of her competitors and was not afraid of taking bold decisions.

If Jaddan Bai made Nargis, similarly, I cannot forget the larger-than-life personality and instantaneously impressive aura of Raj Kapoor's genius father, Prithvi Raj Kapoor, who inspired several subsequent generations of the Kapoor dynasty and impacted the Kapoor clan of Peshawar for generations. There is no denying the fact that the Nargis-Raj Kapoor duo entertained countless cinema-goers for nearly a decade, and long after they were separated, gone from this world, they still keep India and the Indian diaspora fully entertained by leaving behind an excellent lineup of 16 evergreen films, which they created for the entertainment of posterity. I particularly admire Nargis and Raj Kapoor's simple language, which is spoken all over the densely populated Indo-Gangetic plains of northern India. It is truly Hindustani—an amalgamation of urban-spoken Hindi and urban-spoken Urdu. Other than the language, their professional brilliance, too, is beyond commendable.

In a flashback, my brain goes back to the sittings of the Constituent Assembly of India in the magnificent British-built Parliament House in New Delhi. An acrimonious debate was going on to choose the national language of independent India. The then Prime Minster of India, Pandit Jawahar Lal Nehru, was a real secularist supporter of the Hindustani language, a combination of Hindi and Urdu, spoken on the streets of all the major metropolises on the basins of the Yamuna and the Ganges, for example, Delhi, Lucknow, Allahabad, Agra, Kanpur, and other large central Indian cities of Bhopal, Indore, Gwalior, Jubbulpore, and Jaipur. The other leader of national stature, Sardar Vallabh Bhai Patel, was supporting Hindi as the national language. Finally, when the debate ended and voting was held in the house, Hindi was chosen by merely a razor-thin difference of one vote. A shocked Nehru was sulking, and so was the cinema-going secular India who had gotten used to hearing Nargis and Raj Kapoorian Hindustani. Pandit Nehru's choice was endorsed by the filmmakers and the movie-goers by overwhelmingly approving the language of, among other countless film stars, the combination of Nargis and Raj Kapoor's spoken language, Hindustani. Although the members of the Parliament chose Hindi, India as a whole affirmed their faith in Nehru's preference for a simpler, nationally spoken language. Even these days, most of the densely populated northern and central India's *lingua franca* is Hindustani, which is also the language of poets, lyricists, and storywriters of countless films. Pandit Jawahar Lal Nehru liked to mingle with leading film stars like Sohrab Modi, Prithvi Raj

Kapoor, Moti Lal, Dilip Kumar, Raj Kapoor, Dev Anand, Nargis, Madhubala, Suraiya, Balraj Sahni, and Nirupa Roy to name a few, all of whom spoke Hindustani. Pakistan's largest city, Karachi, which used to be a Sindhi-speaking city before August 1947, also speaks Hindustani (Urdu) these days. Even the second language of Pakistani Punjab's capital, Lahore, is akin to Hindustani.

Another aspect of Nargis-Raj Kapoor films that stood out to me was that they used to be remarkably less violent and much less cruel to the hero and heroine. Rich in entertainment, these films did remarkably well at the box office. A lot of the other producers did exactly the opposite, though.

Music, too, has played a great role in all the Nargis-Raj Kapoor hit films. For most of these films, the Shanker-Jaikishan duo deserves a lot of credit, but in the 1952 film *Ashiana*, the music composed by Madan Mohan for the same actor combination also left its mark remarkably well.

The author with Lata Mangeshkar, music director Jaikishan and poet Hasrat Jaipuri

Pre-Nargis-Raj Kapoor Indian Film Scene

Just like most of Europe and the USA, India made a transition from silent movies to black and white talkies in 1931, with the first-ever Hindustani language talkie named *Alam Ara*. After that, there was a spurt in the production of Hindustani movies. Regional talking cinema also proliferated with films made in Bengali, Tamil, Marathi, and Punjabi.

Kundan Lal Saigal

India's first male superstar in the film industry was the late Kundan Lal Saigal. He was a Punjabi, born in Jammu—the second largest city of the erstwhile state of Jammu and Kashmir. Otherwise, he hailed from Jullundur (now Jalandhar) in the eastern part of Punjab. Compared to others of his time, he was a great actor and an even greater singer. He ruled the Indian 'talking cinema' in its infancy, from 1932 to early 1947, and was professionally based in the then-largest city of Calcutta (now

Kolkata), which also happened to be the first prominent centre of the Indian film industry. In the mid-1940s, the focus of the north Indian film industry started converging on Mumbai, which developed into the primary centre of the Hindi or Urdu film industry. Kundan Lal Saigal had a rich and heavy male voice, quite naturally suited to be a great singer. He hardly ever needed any rehearsal for his recording sessions, and no elaborate orchestra was required as an accompaniment either. Although he was immensely admired for his qualities of head and heart by all his female co-actors, considering the characteristics of the conservative Indian society of those years, it is to his achievement that his name was not involved in any scandals. The storyline of the films in his era moved at an awfully slow pace, and his temperament was perfectly in sync with that slow pace.

A film titled *Devdas* (1936) was made during the days of K. L. Saigal and was, again, remade during the 1950s with Dilip Kumar as the male leading actor. The opinion of cinema-goers differs widely. The contemporaries of K. L. Saigal liked his version of the movie, whereas fans of Dilip Kumar liked the

one made in the 1950s. Even the music of the two was vastly different. Clearly, within a decade, the tastes of cinema-goers had changed a whole lot, and it was hard to keep pace with the rapidly changing tastes of the public.

After K. L. Saigal's untimely death in the winter of 1947, no actor or singer could claim to fill the vacuum left by his sudden disappearance from the movie scene. Two otherwise highly regarded singers, Mukesh and C. H. Atma, tried to copy his unique style of singing, but none could come even close to his exalted stature. A highly acclaimed Hindustani film and ghazal singer, Talat Mahmood, often referred to him as the greatest film singer of all time who could never be replicated. Afterwards, the film industry made rapid strides, and many great actors emerged who ruled the film world and departed, but the complete dominance enjoyed by K. L. Saigal during the early days of Indian cinema was indeed unique. No single male actor and singer after him could occupy the special place that he enjoyed. All his successors, barring Kishore Kumar, ended up being playback singers only. Talat Mahmood was a serious contender for acting roles in films. He tried his luck in several movies, including *Raj Laxmi* (1945), *Tum Aur Main* (1947), *Sampatti* (1949), *Aaram* (1951), *Thokar* (1953), *Dil-e-Nadaan* (1953), *Daak Babu* (1954), *Waris* (1954), *Raftar* (1955), *Diwali Ki Raat* (1956), *Ek Gaon Ki Kahani* (1957), *Lala Rukh* (1958), *Maalik* (1958), and *Sone Ki Chidiya* (1958). His heroines, especially Suraiya, Shyama, and Shashikala, liked him for the decent, well-mannered, and sophisticated actor that he was. The comedian-actor, Kishore Kumar, however, turned out to be, indeed, two-in-one.

Dilip Kumar: The Hero of Sad and Serious Roles

Dilip Kumar (childhood name Yusuf Khan) was, perhaps, the most durable and talented actor post-K. L. Saigal, in the Hindi or Urdu film industry. He, too, like Saigal, was an actor cut out for profound and sad roles whose presence on the screen meant a thundering box office success of the film. Most of the movies during the 1940s–70s, in which Dilip Kumar starred, had tragic scenes and lots of torture. Dilip Kumar could admirably fit into these tragic roles. He enjoyed a great command over the Urdu language, the *lingua franca* of Indian cinema from the 1930s–60s. His repeated pairing with India's full-of-charm and highly acclaimed actress, Madhubala—a ravishing beauty hailing from the North West Frontier Province—was the talk of the Indian film world, but this highly talented pair was surprisingly eclipsed at the box office by the maverick duo of Nargis and Raj Kapoor.

Dilip Kumar paired successfully with India's top singer-actress Noor Jehan in the film *Jugnu* (1947) before she went back to Lahore after the creation of Pakistan. Dilip Kumar, too, was urged to leave for the newly-created country, but he did not agree. His heart and soul were in secular India. He acted opposite Kamini Kaushal in a patriotic film *Shaheed* in 1948. It became a superhit. He also acted opposite another superstar, Suraiya—an actress with a silken soft singing voice. Among the others that he starred opposite were Suchitra Sen, Nimmi, Meena Kumari, Munawar Sultana, Nargis, and Vyjayanthimala, to name a few.

Dilip Kumar was capable of carrying any film alone on his broad shoulders. He was the proverbial tragedy king of the Indian film industry. Some of his finest and most popular films include *Jawar Bhata* (1944), *Milan* (1946), *Jugnu* (1947), *Shaheed* (1948), *Mela* (1948), *Nadiya Ke Paar* (1948), *Andaz*

(1949), *Shabnam* (1949), *Babul* (1950), *Aarzoo* (1950), *Jogan* (1950), *Tarana* (1951), *Deedar* (1951), *Aan* (1952), *Sangdil* (1952), *Footpath* (1953), *Amar* (1954), *Devdas* (1955), *Azaad* (1955), *Insaniyat* (1955), *Naya Daur* (1957), *Musafir* (1957), *Mughal-e-Azam* (1960), *Ganga Jamuna* (1961), *Leader* (1964), *Ram Aur Shyam* (1967), *Dastaan* (1972), *Kanoon Apna Apna* (1989), and *Saudagar* (1991). In all these films, not one of his acting performances could be considered ordinary or below par. His romantic role in the most expensive historic extravaganza of its time, *Mughal-e-Azam* (1960), will be remembered forever by posterity.

It was around 2000 that his health started deteriorating fast. For a very long time, he was the most sought-after bachelor who, on one or the other pretext, kept postponing his marriage. Finally, when his youth was almost over, he tied the knot with the ravishing beauty Saira Bano, daughter of the legendary actor Naseem Bano. Saira Bano's love and tender care served him remarkably well in his old age when he needed care the most. She was present day and night at his bedside and was with him when he breathed his last in 2021. Dilip Kumar, beyond doubt, dedicated his entire life to making the Indian film industry artistically richer.

Dev Anand: The Handsome, Sensuous, and Playful Actor

During the immediate post-Saigal years, Dilip Kumar was accepted as the most brilliant and profound actor meant for sad and serious roles, but Raj Kapoor's immediate rival as a showman was none other than another Punjabi actor—Dev Anand of Gurdaspur district in East Punjab. Dev Anand was a strikingly handsome and thinly built actor with an exclusive landmark style of acting. Some of India's leading ladies considered him outrightly seductive. He, by his admission, was often in love with some lady or the other who used to be featured opposite him or was aspiring to act opposite him. Average cinema-goers did not believe in his countless love stories, but they appreciated his frankness in talking about his open and hidden love affairs.

By his admission, he was at one time genuinely in love with a very popular acting and singing star, Suraiya, during the early years of his acting career. The two love birds constituted a highly romantic couple in films like *Vidya* (1948), *Jeet* (1949), *Shair* (1949), *Afsar* (1950), *Nili* (1950), *Do Sitare* (1951), and *Sanam* (1951) during a short span of three years. If allowed to perform unhindered and at liberty without any communal, social, and religious restrictions imposed by the women who were her seniors, the Suraiya-Dev Anand pair could have surpassed the success record created by the pair of Nargis and Raj Kapoor, who, in every film, looked like a perfectly at ease pair tailor-made for each other. Their education in elite schools in British India was one of their common links, which eventually made them an ideal pair in perfect unison with each other's talents. Years later, Dev Anand was paired with actress Nutan in the film *Paying Guest* (1957). His roles in films like *Baazi* (1951), *Hum Dono*

(1961), *Jab Pyaar Kisise Hota Hai* (1961), *Tere Ghar Ke Saamne* (1963), and *Guide* (1965) earned him critical appreciation from the elite and tabloid press as well as the man on the street and intelligentsia of independent India.

After their painful breakup, for none of their faults, both Dev Anand and Suraiya were badly jolted. Suraiya decided not to get married all her life, but Dev Anand had no emotional attachment to any female actor, and because of this, he started taking too much liberty in his ventures opposite new actors looking for work. He was responsible for making the careers of several actresses. At one time, he was infatuated by the overall charm of Zeenat Aman, and she did not disappoint him with her bold portrayals in freewheeling roles. Dev Anand was adjudged by many as the Indian version of evergreen Hollywood actors Gregory Peck or Rock Hudson.

Prithvi Raj Kapoor: The Head of the Kapoor Clan

Raj Kapoor's father, Prithvi Raj Kapoor, had a great personality and was cut out for big roles. He was a role model for the entire Kapoor clan. His influential coat-tails were so long, wide, and deep that his cousins, distant relatives, and their progeny, too, tried to emulate his example. Prithvi Raj Kapoor was born on 3 November 1906 in the fast-growing town of Samundri, in the equally fast-growing Lyallpur district of the Multan division of Punjab, now in Pakistan. To gauge his level of talent for acting, watching just three of his films is enough—*Sikandar* (1941), *Mughal-e-Azam* (1960), and *Nanak Naam Jahaz Hai* (1969), the last one being a Punjabi film. *Mughal-e-Azam* (1960) was the most expensive masterpiece of its time, showcasing the finest specimens of conversational Urdu. *Nanak Naam Jahaz* (1969) *Hai* was an excellent example of standard (Central) Lahori or

Amritsari Punjabi dominating the province before 1947. This film won the 1970 National Film Award for Best Feature Film in Punjabi and National Film Award for Best Music Direction.

Prithvi Raj Kapoor's Prithvi Theatre was founded in 1944 in Mumbai. It was the forerunner of R. K. Theatre. This is the place where all the Kapoors and several other stars honed their skills in professional acting.

Two of the lesser-known Raj Kapoor siblings, Shammi Kapoor and Shashi Kapoor, did not put on flop shows either. For instance, Shammi Kapoor acted in serious roles in films like *Laila Majnu* (1953), *Mirza Sahiban* (1957), *Shama Parwana* (1954), and *Rangeen Raatein* (1956). But during the '60s, in films like *Junglee* (1961), *Professor* (1962), and *Dil Tera Deevana* (1962), he played glamorous and flamboyant roles. However, they could not leave as much of a lasting footprint on the Bollywood film industry as the Nargis-Raj Kapoor films during their golden period from 1948–56.

Raj Kapoor

The Kapoor Dynasty and Raj Kapoor's Early Life

Raj Kapoor was born in a typical well-to-do urban Punjabi Khatri *Rais* (rich) Hindu family of Western Punjab, a region dominated by Muslims professing faith in the Sunni sect. His father, Prithvi Raj Kapoor, was a handsome, tall, and strongly-built Punjabi who was born in an affluent Rai Bahadur family of Peshawar, temporarily relocated in Samundri Town, Samundri Tehsil, Lyallpur district of Multan division of British India's Punjab Province. At the time of the birth of Raj Kapoor, the family was back in their ancestral town of Peshawar, the capital city in the North West Frontier Province (now Khyber Pakhtunkhwa) from where they hailed in the past and from where their family imbibed some influence of the Hindko dialect of the Punjabi language, which is spoken by the Punjabis of the Peshawar region. I mention this to distinguish their culture from other cultures in a vast country. Raj Kapoor's mother's name was Ram Sarani Devi Kapoor. She was a grand, though uneducated, lady, generous to the core and an ideal counterfoil for a domineering husband. As a housewife, she raised the kids as properly as she could. This family originally hailed from Central Punjab, situated around the provincial capital, Lahore, but they kept moving and later settled in the Peshawar area, where they were treated with awe and respect meant for the highly respected landed elite.

Raj Kapoor's grandfather was Rai Bahadur Basheshwar Nath Kapoor, and his great-grandfather was Rai Bahadur Keshav Nath Kapoor. His esteemed great-great-grandfather was Dewan Murli Mal Kapoor. They were a big, well-to-do clan, commanding great respect in their area. The Hindus and Sikhs were a very insignificant minority all over North West Frontier Province, but they were financially and socially muchmore influential than the numerical majority of the Sunni Islamic community.

The Pathans or the Pashtoons (Pakhtoons) were, and still are, regarded as the men of their word. If they make a promise, they fulfil it even at the cost of their life. However, when the communal relations between the Muslims and the Hindus became embittered in 1947, all the centuries-old goodwill vanished in a matter of days, and the minorities were massacred in absolute cold blood. The worst riots occurred in the North West Frontier Province and the neighbouring areas of Swat, Mirpur, Muzaffarabad, and Baltistan, where the Hindus and Sikhs were a tiny minority. To give him the finest education, young Raj Kapoor was moved to the safety of the United Provinces in North Central India, where the Hindus constituted a brute majority.

The spoken language of the Frontier-based Kapoor clan was standard Punjabi spoken in Central Punjab's Lahore division and some areas of adjoining districts like Lyallpur and Montgomery of neighbouring Multan division and in the Gujarat district of the Rawalpindi division. The rest of the Rawalpindi division spoke the Pothohari dialect. A majority of Khatri caste Hindus stayed in the politically important central districts of Punjab around Lahore. Had young Raj Kapoor stayed in the Peshawar area during the days of his schooling, his spoken dialect would have been Hindko Punjabi, a dialect that is quite close to the Pothohari dialect of the Rawalpindi division.

Other than the Kapoors, there was another top-class film industry-related family with a *rais* background. This was music director Madan Mohan's family. His father was Rai Bahadur Chuni Lal of Chakwal town in Jhelum district, located within the Rawalpindi division of Western Punjab. Although Madan Mohan was born in Iraq—some say in Erbil (Iraqi Kurdistan), and others say in Baghdad—after a few years, they returned to Punjab Province in British India and later settled in Mumbai. The Kapoors were associated with the agricultural profession and probably had no interaction with the Chakwal Kohlis, who had expertise in accounts and stayed for a long time in Muslim-dominated Iraq.

Prithvi Raj Kapoor was a pioneer in India's theatre movement and was perpetually on the move with his drama crew. In his native Punjab, most plays were staged in the twin-rich cities of Lahore and Amritsar. Punjab's oldest theatre, Chitra, in Amritsar, hosted several shows of Prithvi Raj Kapoor's group. Prithvi Raj Kapoor, even in his childhood, had a strong inclination for acting in the film industry and theatre, and he hopped, unhesitatingly, between the theatre and film industry. During his school and college days, he participated in several plays. After attaining adulthood, Prithvi Raj Kapoor, possessing a deep voice, became more famous as a pioneering personality of theatre rather than cinema. They lived in a huge and sprawling house called the Kapoor Haveli in Peshawar, where Raj Kapoor was born as the first child of Prithvi Raj Kapoor.

It has been reliably learnt that the famous Kapoor Haveli in a commercial area of Peshawar has remained by and large unchanged even seven decades after the creation of Pakistan and the exchange of population. This haveli is now being vacated from its post-partition occupiers and being restored by the Government of Pakistan to give it the look of a tourist attraction. Some of the antique memorabilia associated with the film industry of India, perhaps, will find a place in this museum. In 1947, the misguided Punjabi and Pathan Muslim youth of the North West Frontier Province violently threw all the Hindus and the Sikhs out of the province. By now, they have realised their Himalayan blunder of 1947 and want to encash the memorabilia associated with the rich and famous Hindu dynasties of pre-partition days.

Raj Kapoor was born in the Dhakki Munawwar Shah area in the Kissakhwani Bazaar region of Peshawar on 14 December 1924. It is just a coincidence that the most popular male playback singer, Mohammad Rafi, was born ten days later, on Christmas Eve of the same year, in the village Kotla Sultan Singh in Amritsar district. Raj Kapoor's exposure to the Peshawari culture was hardly any when he was moved out of the province for schooling in an elite institution. His early schooling took place in an English medium elite school, the Colonel Brown Cambridge School in Dehradun in the United Provinces. It can be concluded that when the time of his cultural development came, he was moved out of the North Western Frontier Province and West Punjab into the Jamuna-Gangetic heartland, where he imbibed a composite culture. He changed several schools. Some part of Raj Kapoor's school age was spent in India's cultural capital of Kolkata, where he was enrolled in the famous St. Xavier's Collegiate School. Subsequently, he studied at Campion School in Mumbai. Moving from school to school in some of the largest cities of the Presidencies of British India built his confidence strongly, and at a young age, he developed enough courage to face the stark realities of life. He had this with him even as a seasoned film producer. His confidence to produce movies on his own and to face financial adversities bravely came from his smart schooling in the elite schools of India and his father's discipline.

His father, Prithvi Raj Kapoor, was highly influenced by the teachings of Guru Nanak Dev *ji*. It was the music director S. Mohinder, who composed the music for a blockbuster Punjabi film, *Nanak Naam Jahaz Hai* (1969) and worked closely with the veteran star Prithvi Raj Kapoor, who shared this bit of information. S. Mohinder told me that Kapoor enjoyed listening to *shabad kirtan* whenever he could get a chance to listen to *Gurbani* in one of the scores of gurdwaras of Mumbai. Even while in Samundri and Peshawar, Prithvi Raj Kapoor loved to listen to *shabad gurbani* being recited in the gurdwaras of Lyallpur district and Peshawar. His visit to Lahore was never complete without his pilgrimage to the Golden Temple in Amritsar.

Raj Kapoor's schooling took place in English and Hindi/Urdu languages. He could speak Hindi fluently, but not the typical Brahminical Sanskritised version of Hindi, and his Urdu was not of the type taught by the maulvis of Lucknow, Allahabad, Delhi, Agra, Rampur, and Aligarh. His language was typical Hindustani spoken on the streets of Delhi, Meerut, Kanpur, Jaipur, Indore, Bhopal, Dehradun, Saharanpur, and Allahabad. He mastered both Devanagari and Persian/Arabic scripts, so he had no difficulty in reading and understanding the scripts in both Urdu and Hindi languages. His weakness in Persian/Arabic scripts was more than adequately compensated by Nargis' command over these Islamic scripts. Raj Kapoor's father was not a staunch Hindu, as explained above. Instead, he had a lot of regard for Buddhism and Islamic religion; therefore, on the whole, the family was a very liberal and secular one. I have been told that within the four walls of their home, the language of interaction in the family was in their mother tongue—Punjabi. On the maternal side, everybody conversed in chaste Punjabi. For a short while, both Raj Kapoor and music director Madan Mohan Kohli studied together in an elite school in Dehradun, but it is surprising that while picking a music director for the Nargis-Raj Kapoor films made under his banner, R. K. Films, he never considered giving a chance to a brilliant fellow Punjabi music director Madan Mohan. Of course, he liked the music of the film *Ashiana* (1952) and so many other films like *Bhai Bhai* (1956), *Railway Platform* (1955), *Gateway of India* (1957), *Jailor* (1958), and *Samundar* (1957), all composed by Madan Mohan. Some of the songs of the film *Ashiana* (1952) in the voices of Talat Mahmood and Lata Mangeshkar have been great hits. One particular song, *Mera Qarar Le Ja*, had become especially popular.

Partition of Punjab and the Creation of Pakistan

Raj Kapoor indirectly read about the flood of refugees crossing from Pakistan to India, especially those associated with the film industry crossing over to Mumbai from Lahore via Karachi and the Wagah border of Amritsar, and their pitiable and penniless entry from almost all the other Western Punjab districts. In Mumbai, he befriended many Punjabis who had been displaced from Pakistan. Although he was a Punjabi, during his lifetime, he did not produce a single Punjabi film. Nor did he act in one. He died at a very young age when he and his fans were not quite well prepared to see his death, and India, as a whole, was not prepared to see him dying so prematurely.

At the time of independence, India was an extremely poor country with huge income disparities. The commonly used slogan of the wealthy people of the country was to help the poor and the needy displaced people from what is now called Pakistan. Even the otherwise ideological Raj Kapoor was himself, not a capitalist. He was extremely sympathetic towards the poor of the country. His films, thus, generally exhibited a socialistic underlying theme. Dilip Kumar also made similar left-leaning films, and these did reasonably well at the box office. Just look at Dilip Kumar's *Naya Daur* (1957) and Raj Kapoor's *Jagte Raho* (1956) and *Boot Polish* (1954).

Raj Kapoor's Early Career in the Film Industry

Neel Kamal, made in 1947, was a dry run for Raj Kapoor's future career as an actor. The female lead was the most beautiful actor of the time, perhaps even of the twentieth century—Madhubala. During those days, to act opposite Madhubala was considered a sure ticket to box office bonanza. Even as a new budding actor, Raj Kapoor did quite well in his debut performance. Since Madhubala had also started acting as a child, her performance was also good. After that, Raj Kapoor put all his eggs in Nargis' basket, who became his constant female companion for the next eight years; other than one-off films like *Boot Polish* (1954) and *Bawre Nain* (1950)—in the latter, the heroine was an Amritsari girl, Geeta Bali.

It can be confidently concluded that as a personal choice, Raj Kapoor, during his most successful and productive years in the film industry, fully enjoyed his assignments in roles opposite

Nargis. He was a medium-statured, skinny man. His height was barely five feet and seven inches. His looks were compatible with Hollywood and British movie stars. His colour complexion was very fair, like an Italian or a French European male. He had blue eyes, which are very rare in India but very common in Europe. He even had a sharp nose and high cheekbones. All this made him stand out in the Indian film industry.

His illustrious father wanted Raj Kapoor to stand on his own feet, which he learned to do at the beginning of his film career. Whereas Dilip Kumar's education was mostly in the vernacular languages, Raj Kapoor learnt a lot of different languages from the British education system and from the Hollywood movies of the time. During his school days, he was extensively exposed to American and other Western music, which made the music of his movies unique. The surprisingly creative pair of music directors Shanker and Jaikishan loved to compose something different from the run-of-the-mill Indian film music directors. Compared to the classical or semi-classical music of the existing music directors, they created some off-the-beaten-track music, which brought name and fame to Nargis-Raj Kapoor movies too. Raj Kapoor's Urdu improved markedly by talking repeatedly with Nargis and by listening to Hasrat Jaipuri's lyrics in simple Urdu. Even Shailendra composed lyrics in conversational Urdu.

Raj Kapoor turned out to be a very intelligent man. He learnt a lot from his experimentation in the film *Aag* (1948) and its failure to generate money. Quite early in his career, he learnt the strength of music in an Indian film. During his best acting years, he persisted with the music-composing duo of Shanker and Jaikishan. Later, when he felt that he must change to the new number one, he switched to Laxmikant-Pyarelal. His last choice of music director was Ravinder Jain, who also succeeded.

When the need arose, Raj Kapoor requested his father to act in his films as well. Through his fiscal strictness, his father, Prithvi Raj Kapoor, made Raj Kapoor financially independent. Hailing from a *rais* Rai Bahadur family, Raj Kapoor could have been a spoiled brat, but he was not. He was fiscally a very wise spender, which was why, after every unsuccessful business venture, he bounced right back.

Copying Charlie Chaplin

Raj Kapoor was a big fan of the British comedian-actor Charlie Chaplin, active in the first half of the twentieth century. In his spare time, he used to stand before a mirror, practising the comedian's mimicry. In several scenes of *Shree 420* (1955), he was seen copying the acting style of Charlie Chaplin, which was liked by Indian cinema-goers, especially those who had had exposure to Western movies. Raj Kapoor also loved the acting of comedian Laurel of the duo of Laurel and Hardy. To generate sympathy for himself, he preferred to dress like Laurel. This type of portrayal amused European cinema-goers as well.

Raj Kapoor Propagated Indian Films Abroad

Raj Kapoor was the first film producer in India who created a market for Indian films outside the Indian subcontinent. Hardly anyone in Russia or the Soviet Union knew Hindi or Urdu, yet Raj Kapoor's films were regarded with the utmost respect in the remote areas of the Soviet Union. In fact, Nargis-Raj Kapoor films found a lucrative market in the Soviet Union and other Eastern European countries. The song from *Shree 420* (1955), *Mera Joota Hai Japani*, became very popular in Eastern Europe.

Another song from the movie *Awaara* (1951), *Awaara Hoon*, became the very first number that got publicly recognised first in Russia and then in the entire Soviet Union. Raj Kapoor was the first Indian cinema personality who, without knowing the Russian language, could relate to the Soviet people. He looked like an Eastern European or Central Asian, as did Nargis. During those days, the Jawaharlal Nehru-led Indian Government was adopting a socialistic pattern of society. Raj Kapoor had no political party affiliation, but he, too, was sympathetic towards the poor and was an outspoken protagonist of socialism or the socialistic pattern of society. Showing an inclination towards left-oriented policies was a fashion in India during those days.

In *Naya Daur* (1957), even the other leading actor, Dilip Kumar, expressed his love for socialism and glorified it throughout the film. India, during the respective Congress regimes before the now-forgotten period of Prime Minister Narasimha Rao, was a die-hard believer in socialism as the state policy. But, even under the slight right of the central administration of Narasimha Rao, India never declared itself as a capitalistic country. Even former Prime Minister Dr. Manmohan Singh, a renowned economist, is not a die-hard protagonist of the American brand of hard and ruthless capitalism. Raj Kapoor was right hence, and to be candid, he may be right even in the future. Poor countries like India are beset with circumstances that linger for decades and not just some years.

Raj Kapoor's Great Satisfaction Due to Nargis' Company

Raj Kapoor had so much respect for his co-star Nargis that in all the films, it was considered a Nargis-Raj Kapoor pairing and not the other way round. Nargis' mother was a famous Hindustani classical singer, Jaddan Bai, who was a Muslim, and her father was a Hindu converted to Islam. Nargis turned out to be a healthy, brainy, and smart child. Before attaining adulthood, she was already seasoned as an actor because of her acting assignments in films as a six-year-old child. Comparatively speaking, Raj Kapoor was a raw hand, only a determined entrepreneur who, most of the time, enjoyed great luck in his ventures. Socially and culturally, both had identical schooling. Both knew English very well, and both had learnt European mannerisms. They were both good swimmers and horse riders. They appreciated good international music, and both were masters of rhythm. Their similarity also lay in the fact that neither was an exceptionally good or trained classical or Western-style freewheeling dancer.

During those early years after the independence of India, speaking chaste Urdu was considered a fashion statement. Jaddan Bai was a highly accomplished orator of Urdu. Thus, since Nargis' childhood, she groomed her thoroughly to speak Urdu authoritatively. Jaddan Bai was partly Punjabi. She was married to a wealthy Punjabi Hindu Brahmin, Uttamchand Mohanchand, who, after marriage, converted to Islam and assumed the Islamic name Abdul Rashid. Jaddan Bai herself was a brilliantly trained classical musician and dancer. Her command over the Urdu language and its Persian and Arabic vocabulary was amazing. She was an excellent trainer, especially for her daughter Nargis, whose acting capabilities dazzled the whole of India and the young neighbouring nation of Pakistan. In a country like Pakistan, where more than 50 per cent of the people speak Punjabi, Urdu was popularised tremendously by Hindustani films like the various Nargis-Raj Kapoor starrer hits as well as movies of actors like Dilip Kumar with Madhubala and Meena Kumari among others. The assured association of Nargis as the unfailing female partner of Raj Kapoor and the support that this fact received from the cinema-going public of India encouraged the latter to build his studio.

R. K. Studios in Andheri, Mumbai

It is surprising that a young actor and film producer, Raj Kapoor, could build his studio in a sprawling complex at a very young age. He made at least some part of each of his films at the R. K. Studios, which was improvised from scratch in 1948, but Raj Kapoor kept expanding it every year as and when money was available until a time came when several other film producers expressed their desire to use it. The studio did well as long as Raj Kapoor was alive. After his death, it appeared to be a victim of neglect. Once, it even caught fire due to a short circuit. Perhaps its wiring had multiple joints and was never upgraded, which might have caused the fire. The loss was worth millions of rupees. The family, at that juncture, could not afford to rebuild it. So, in 2017, the family sold it. All R. K. movies were filmed primarily at this venue. In addition to movie shootings, this studio was the venue of a lot of lavish Bollywood parties which the bigwigs attended.

Nargis

Early Life of Nargis

Nargis was born on 1 June 1929 in Kolkata, the largest metropolis of India and the then leading film city—much ahead of Mumbai. This great city was the new home of Nargis' parents. Nargis was a remarkably pretty child with well-chiselled Aryan features—a sharp nose, high cheekbones, a large upper jaw, a wide opening mouth, and a fair complexion. These features made her look like the international actress Gina Lollobrigida or Elizabeth Taylor. Nargis received the best possible education her parents could arrange for her in the most cultured and civilised city of Kolkata.

Most of her education in film acting was practically attained as a child star in films. From her childhood, she was an excellent candidate for becoming an actress. Since birth, Nargis was exposed to her mother's sweet voice and sublime music. So, the development of good taste in music was what she imbibed since her childhood. Nargis started acting as a child. Her first role as a child actor came when she was only six. It was the 1935 film, *Talash-E-Haq*. In 1936, she acted in *Madam Fashion*, and in 1937, *Moti ka Haar*. Each of her roles taught her something new. She was one of the rare actors who happened to be quite at home with both English and Urdu.

Her next film came after a gap of five years when she acted in *Parda Nasheen* in 1942. After that, in 1943, she played a serious role as an adult in the film *Taqdeer*. Although she was still a teenager, her acting was mature. In 1944, she acted in *Aan Baan* and in 1945, in *Humayun*, with a significant role in the latter. Girls during her time could perform the roles of adults at a much earlier age than their real adult age. This was true of her contemporary female actors like Suraiya and Madhubala as well. Her mother was instrumental in selecting the roles that she was supposed to undertake. Her role in the film *Mela* (1948) is considered one of her finest serious roles in the early movies she did at the time. In this film, Dilip Kumar was featured as the leading male actor. The music was composed by music director Naushad Ali—one of the best in the business. The female voice who did the playback singing for Nargis was that of Shamshad Begum. Shamshad Begum was born in Lahore and was a part of Master Ghulam Haider's group of musicians after she shifted to Mumbai. Shamshad Begum did very well in all of her assignments, including those of playback singing for Nargis. Her performance was at par with that of a classically trained singer. However, the soft and soothing sweetness in the voice of the newly found gem, Lata Mangeshkar, was a breed apart. Within a period of less than a year after her discovery, Begum became the choice of music director, Husan Lal-Bhagat Ram, the most in-demand pair of music directors in 1949–50. She was also the first choice of Raj Kapoor's pick for music director, the duo of Shanker and Jaikishan, who, as mentioned above, made the debut of their musical journey with the Nargis and Raj Kapoor starrer film *Barsaat* (1949). Perhaps, after *Mela* (1948), *Aag*

(1948), *Babul* (1950), and *Deedar* (1951), Shamshad Begum's voice was not used for playback singing assignments in the case of Nargis.

Nargis and Her Fluffy Hair-styling

Nargis was very non-compromising about her hair styling. She knew that she had a long and narrow face. So, she selected a European layered and fluffy hairstyle, which enhanced the appeal of her personality. After shooting scenes depicting heavy downpours and stormy weather, where she was drenched, and her hairstyle was spoiled, she preferred to rush to her hairstyle expert to restore the original look. Nargis, for the best years of her acting career, did not put on weight, but she had conspicuously broad shoulders like those of athletes. This was evident from her looks in movies like *Mela* (1948), *Anokha Pyar* (1948), and *Aag* (1948), and even those in *Chori Chori* (1956) and *Mother India* (1957). Nargis, due to her exceptional success rate, was also the best-paid female actor of her time, though she never bargained with Raj Kapoor. From the point of view of the expression of grief and deep emotions, Nargis was the best in the business. Also, from the point of view of acting ability and facial expression, she had no equal. Later, only Meena Kumari could match her hold over the Urdu language and expression of emotions.

Nargis: Dominating the Male Stars

Indian cinema, most of the time, has been dominated by male actors. It is true even today, but the charismatic Nargis was an exception who, on the strength of her acting talent, elocution, spontaneity, and command over the Urdu language, played an equal, if not far superior role to her male stars. The experts in the Indian film industry rated her way above her competition. In every film, she created a special place for herself by dint of her brilliance. Compared to the average male stars of the Indian film industry, Nargis was a far superior actress with a beautiful romantic voice and amazing dialogue delivery.

She was also a much bolder actor than her contemporaries and could face any ticklish situation with utmost confidence. She allowed the producers and directors to do more experimentation with the movie script and screenplay. In two of her earliest films—*Mela* (1948), opposite Dilip Kumar, and *Aag* (1948), opposite Raj Kapoor—she amply gave convincing proof of her cinematic brilliance, which she reinforced in *Babul* (1950) and *Deedar* (1951) while acting opposite Dilip Kumar. Raj Kapoor, of course, made her the only partner for almost all the pictures from 1948 till their painful breakup in 1956 during the time of the release of their blockbuster film, *Chori Chori* (1956). Nargis also made it clear to all who signed her for their films to sign Raj Kapoor for the male lead.

Nargis-Raj Kapoor

When Raj Kapoor started his film career, Nargis, on the strength of her childhood roles as an extra in several films, was already a pro in film roles. From the point of view of talent, she was miles ahead of her competitors. She was the quickest decision-maker and a fast learner in difficult situations. Raj Kapoor admired Nargis' unique acting skills. Respect generates love, and it was evident that Raj Kapoor had it in plenty for Nargis. While advertising on behalf of the acting pair and talking among his friends, Raj Kapoor invariably mentioned the name of Nargis ahead of him.

On the other hand, without disclosing it in public, Nargis also developed a tremendous appreciation for Raj Kapoor's resilience, forthrightness, and spontaneity. She found him to be a sort of maverick and worthy of admiration. After working closely with brilliant male actors in films like *Andaz* (1949), Nargis did two more films – *Babul* (1950) and *Deedar* (1951) – with the then leader of the pack of film heroes, Dilip Kumar. However, after *Andaz* (1949), barring a couple of other films, she almost abandoned Dilip Kumar. Dilip Kumar, on the other hand, had a huge lineup of female actors to work with, and his films were doing reasonably well—so he remained unfazed through the ups and downs of his films. He, in fact, on the strength of his overall acting abilities, was much in demand.

After working closely with Nargis, Raj Kapoor's search for a heroine was all but over. The same appeared true of Nargis, too. In almost all their romantic episodes, Nargis appeared to be genuinely in love with Raj Kapoor. The two achieved plenty of milestone roles together. This gave more strength to their bond and mutual adoration, and their appreciation for each other grew. The reviews by experts, including the most prestigious *Filmfare* and *Screen*, were also extremely flattering. They were mobbed all the time by those who came to see them shoot for the films. They acted together and, during shooting sessions, chatted and ate together.

Raj Kapoor was a Hindu by birth but not a rigid old-fashioned ritualist. On the other side, Nargis was a Muslim, but just like her mother, she was a modernist—highly liberal and a thoroughly open-minded Muslim. All the films in which they acted together, more or less, had Hindu themes, and the names of the characters they portrayed were Hindu as well. Like a seasoned professional, Nargis had no objection to these

Hindu characters that she was given to portray; rather, she enjoyed the preponderance of rituals that she was made to perform. Although in her childhood roles, she acted as a Muslim girl most of the time, as an adult, she never insisted on playing Islamic roles. This quality of Nargis is, most definitely, worthy of appreciation.

Before his close friendship and professional association with Nargis, Raj Kapoor acted opposite several brilliant actors, but the kind of pleasure and satisfaction he drew from his decade-long closeness with Nargis, was not present with other female actors of that period, even in the post-Nargis era. It would not be wrong to assume that from 1948 to 1956, he spent more high-quality time in the company of Nargis than with his real-life spouse, Krishna Kapoor, who was the sister of actor Prem Nath and comedian Rajinder Nath. The Prem Nath family hailed from the North West Frontier of Pakistan and were distant relatives of the Kapoors.

The temperaments of Nargis and Raj Kapoor were also identical. They were selfless and helpful towards each other. However, when it came to music, Raj Kapoor liked Shanker and Jaikishan's work, but Nargis had a more diverse choice. From her films, it can be concluded that she liked the music compositions of Anil Biswas, Madan Mohan, Naushad, Sajjad Hussain, Sachin Dev Burman, Jai Dev, and Shyam Sunder, to name a few, but on Shanker-Jaikishan, they both concurred.

Raj Kapoor always kept his adoration and feelings for Nargis under wraps. This kept many controversies at bay. On the other hand, from the utter sincerity in acting portrayed by Nargis in the romantic scenes enacted opposite Raj Kapoor, it could be easily made out that she was completely in love with him. This was noticed in the song sequences of at least three films—*Barsaat* (1949), *Awaara* (1951), and *Shree 420* (1955). Raj Kapoor thought that with Nargis firmly by his side, he had great room for experimentation in his ventures, including the enactment of the death of the hero. He probably was unaware of the ultra-conservative temperament of the cinema-going Indian public, which was unable to see their favourite hero contracting a highly dreadful disease like tuberculosis and eventually dying of it, as portrayed in the film *Aah* (1953).

Their sudden breakup was not a joke. It was a watershed event in the history of the Indian film industry. It can be observed from Nargis' ecstatic and highly emotional acting opposite Raj Kapoor that she devoted herself wholeheartedly to him. She sincerely wanted to marry him. Once, she even dared to meet Mumbai Province's Chief Minister Morarji Desai to find a way out for Raj Kapoor to marry her and stay married to two women simultaneously. However, after receiving a blunt rebuff, she gathered the courage to break her professional relationship with Raj Kapoor too. It was a bold decision, which hurt both of them equally and resulted in the ruin of their health, too.

Both Nargis and Raj Kapoor initially handled the situation with great patience and courage, but no one knew how much pain and agony each of them was going through. Nargis decided to say goodbye to her film career after a stellar role in her 1957 film *Mother India,* which attracted nationwide attention and a few other movies like *Lajwanti* (1958) and *Adalat (1958)*.

For Raj Kapoor, his film career was an inspiration for the rest of the Mumbai-based Kapoor dynasty and many more. After the release of the film *Barsaat* in 1949, the brand name Nargis-Raj Kapoor became synonymous with box office success. That made the task of the release of their films very easy in all the film exhibition circuits of India.

The assured market in every film exhibition circuit all over India gave immense encouragement to Raj Kapoor. The East Punjab Circuit consisted of the erstwhile state of Jammu and Kashmir, Himachal Pradesh, and Punjab (including the present state of Haryana). Amritsar was the biggest and the most cinema-loving city in this circuit, with the largest number of cinema houses. Nargis-Raj Kapoor films often celebrated their silver jubilees in the finest cinemas of this city. The Delhi and Uttar Pradesh circuit was the largest of the circuits for Hindi-Urdu films. Delhi was its largest city, and Kanpur and Lucknow were the other two major cities. All these cities were virtually gold mines for Nargis-Raj Kapoor films. Mumbai, Kolkata, Central India, and Rajasthan were the other important areas and lucrative territories for the Nargis-Raj Kapoor brand. Most of their films did markedly well in every circuit. In Pakistan, both of the largest cities – Karachi and Lahore – gave good business to Nargis-Raj Kapoor films, but overall, Dilip Kumar starrer movies did quite good business across Pakistan. In the film *Lahore,* Nargis completely eclipsed the established actor Karan Diwan. Several other mediocre actors were overawed by the cult stature that Nargis had attained. She had a much better schooling, and her film roles as a child helped her career a great deal. Her mother was a strong and bold woman, and Nargis truly imbibed her genes. If Nargis could go all out to make R. K. films a big success, she could bluntly put her foot down when it came to breaking all the bonds with Raj Kapoor. Her resolve was firm as a rock. When she decided to marry Sunil Dutt, she proved in her married life to be the most faithful wife. Sunil Dutt virtually worshipped his wife and did all that was required for her treatment for cancer in the most expensive country in the world, the USA.

The Two Heartthrobs

After seeing years of an unbroken bond, Raj Kapoor considered himself to be a happy-go-lucky person who was also sure of the fact that Nargis would, under no circumstances, dare to abandon him. A lot was in store.

In 1957, soon after the release of *Chori Chori* (1956), Nargis, without the knowledge of Raj Kapoor, signed as the leading lady for the ambitiously conceptualised idealistic film *Mother India*. Normally, before signing any film contract, she used to take Raj Kapoor into confidence, but this was not the case for this important film. It appears something significant had happened between them, which led to the sudden souring of a close relationship. Nargis was desperate to marry Raj Kapoor, and he was being evasive. Since 1948, she had spent time with him in perfect unison—so much so that they were considered a 'virtual' couple. All these years, both had acted together on numerous occasions and had taken each other for granted. Since in professional life, they both got along so well, and it appeared that Nargis did not expect a 'no' from Raj Kapoor to her proposal to get married. Perhaps Raj Kapoor also did not realise that

Nargis was fast approaching her later 20s. During that time, early marriages were the norm. The pressure to get married, internalised or from outside, may have weighed too heavily on the young actor's heart than Raj Kapoor realised. Hence, he showed reluctance to any serious commitment towards Nargis. It is also important to note that at that time, Raj Kapoor was already a married man. His spouse, Krishna Kapoor, was a decent lady from the same community as he was, and they had three children together—whom they both loved very much.

Nargis' bold decision to break the relationship shocked Raj Kapoor and all their well-wishers. The cinema-going public took it as a rude shock. In his day-to-day life, Raj Kapoor tried to show to the world that he was unfazed, but internally, from his later life behaviour, including excessive drinking, it became clear that he was psychologically shattered. Nargis decided to focus wholeheartedly on her superlative performance in the film *Mother India* (1957), and she, too, appeared unfazed, but as time passed, perhaps, the scars of her separation deepened. Perhaps she also felt nostalgic about the best days and years spent in Raj Kapoor's company. People wanted them to bury the hatchet and work together. After all, they had done 16 films together. However, what had happened was irreversible.

Contemporaries Post-Nargis-Raj Kapoor Split

During the three decades post-independence, hundreds of Hindi or Urdu films were churned out by the Indian film industry using numerous permutations and combinations. Indian film industry gained several male stars who were not only popular but also had the acting calibre like Shyam, Ashok Kumar, Motilal, Bharat Bhushan, Pradeep Kumar, Prem Nath, Balraj Sahni,

Kishore Sahu, Ajit, Rajinder Kumar, Raj Kumar, Rehman, Anwar Hussain, Dharmendra, Sunil Dutt, Rajesh Khanna, Vinod Khanna, Shammi Kapoor, Rishi Kapoor, Anil Kapoor, and Jitendra to name a few. They came to the cinema screen to grace the Indian film industry, each in their own specific way. They were quite talented in their own right. They were all paired with an assortment of brilliant contemporary female actors, but none of the pairs proved to be as long-lasting and popular as the pair of Nargis and Raj Kapoor during their heydays.

The best female actors of the pre and post Nargis era included a fine lineup of stars like Durga Khote, Naseem Bano, Mumtaz Shanti, Madhubala, Suraiya, Nalini Jayawant, Begum Para, Veena, Nigar Sultana, Nimmi, Meena Shori, Nutan, Tanuja, Nirupa Roy, Meena Kumari, Vyjayanthimala, Kamini Kaushal, Munawar Sultana, Bina Rai, Asha Mathur, Geeta Bali, Shashikala, Nishi, Shyama, Sheela Ramani, Purnima, Chand Usmani, Padmini, Raagini, B. Saroja Devi, Nadira, Usha Kiran, Suchitra Sen, Mumtaz, Rati Agnihotri, Rekha, Raakhi, Waheeda Rehman, Raj Shri, and Padmini to name a few. They were all brilliant, but none of them gained anything substantial from the brilliance of scores of male partners they starred opposite. Although India's officially accepted national game is hockey, in reality, India loves just two things—cricket as a sport and films as a mode of entertainment.

Nargis' Marriage and Her Loss of Interest in the Film Industry

After *Mother India* (1957), the opportunity to get married knocked at Nargis' door. During the shooting of the film, a bush fire at one of the shooting spots went out of control. Nargis was caught in the middle of the devastating inferno from which it was impossible to get out on her own. A young and physically strong, handsome Punjabi refugee actor from Pakistan, Sunil Dutt, was acting as her son. Without caring a bit for his safety, he jumped into the fire, lifted her, and, in a jiffy, darted out of the fire. Sunil Dutt's face was badly burnt, and Nargis visited him every day to take personal care of him in the hospital.

What he had done had been an act of uncommon daredevilry. Nargis was profoundly touched by this exceptionally courageous act. Sunil Dutt was quite new to the Hindi-Urdu film industry. He was from the Jhelum district of Rawalpindi division of Western Punjab. His spoken mother language was a mixture of standard Punjabi spoken in the Lahore division and the Pothohari dialect of Punjabi spoken in the Rawalpindi division. He had learnt reading and writing Urdu in his younger days, but his accent of Urdu was not the best. The imperfections in his pronunciation of Urdu vocabulary can be found in his first movie, *Railway Platform* (1955). His imperfections were noticed easily during the making of *Mother India* (1957) as well, even though Nargis had helped him to improve it. For Sunil Dutt, it was a lifelong learning experience. In his later movies, his Urdu improved markedly.

After her miraculous rescue, Nargis was extremely thankful to Sunil Dutt. Some think that she was the first to propose to Sunil Dutt to get tied into a marital bond. Others believe he proposed marriage to Nargis. For the common person, it does not matter who made the first proposal, but it is obvious that there was no hesitation from the other side. So they got married in a simple wedding ceremony and settled down as husband and wife. Sunil Dutt was a perfect gentleman and a caring life partner. He never gave Nargis a chance to be angry or to dissent.

There was no doubt that Nargis was a great actress. For her stellar role in *Mother India* (1957), she received the coveted Filmfare Award for Best Actress of the year 1958. After doing a couple of films like *Lajwanti* (1958) and *Adalat* (1958), she took a vacation from her career as an actor for a few years. Her next big role came in *Raat Aur Din* in 1967. Once again, the music was composed by Shanker and Jaikishan, and it turned out to be an outstanding listening experience.

This marriage, to a great extent, freed Nargis from her career in acting. Sunil Dutt proved to be an excellent husband at every step. Nargis wanted to focus on her family. Sanjay Dutt was the first child born to the couple. Both parents wanted to make him a promising actor, but despite plenty of talent, luck did not favour Sanjay Dutt as much. Perhaps he hung around with the local youth of Mumbai too frequently. Making friends is no crime, but his career needed better command over urban-spoken Hindi. His acting was good, but his language was a strange mixture of Hindi, Urdu, and Marathi. Such a language may do well in the back alleys of Mumbai, Pune, and Bhiwandi but not in the Indo-Gangetic heartlands of northern India, where his market was.

Somehow, both Nargis and Sunil Dutt could not pay enough attention to their son's linguistic training. Sanjay Dutt's acting, openness, and friendly nature were appreciated, but it felt like his unconventional amalgam of languages could not be accepted by the masses. The couple's first daughter, Priya Dutt, chose to become a politician and did reasonably well by getting elected to the Parliament to fill the vacuum left by her father, Sunil Dutt's sudden death.

After getting married, Nargis started putting on weight. It was noticed in the film *Raat Aur Din* (1967).

Immediately after the break up with Nargis, Raj Kapoor got busy proving that he is a force to reckon with within the film industry. He did an average actor's role in *Main Nashe Mein Hoon* (1959). He did quite well opposite Nutan in the 1959 film *Anari*. Nutan proved to be a highly entertaining actor, and Raj Kapoor was great as usual. But during the 1960s, he, too, started putting on weight. His films *Dulha Dulhan* (1964) opposite Sadhna, *Around the World* (1966) opposite Raj Shree, and *Sapnon Ka Saudagar* (1968) opposite Hema Malini failed at the box office. His out-of-shape belly was partly to blame.

Nargis-Raj Kapoor Break up: Sadness in Pakistan

The Government of Pakistan had long since banned the screening of Indian movies in cinema halls all over the country and Indian music at Radio Pakistan stations as well. Yet, the typical cinema-goers in cities like Karachi, Hyderabad Sindh, Nawabshah, and Lahore followed the happenings in the Indian film industry very minutely. Through regular smuggling channels, with the epicentre in Amritsar, they could smuggle Indian movies and watch all of them. The sudden breakup between Nargis and Raj Kapoor sent shock waves in Pakistan as well. When *Aah* (1953) flopped in India, it was the Pakistani market which helped in its revival. I liked *Aah*'s music so much that I saw it nine times in the theatres! There must be many like me who watched it time and again. All over the Soviet Union, songs like *Awaara Hoon* and *Mera Joota Hai Japani* outlived the era of Nargis and Raj Kapoor by decades. Although Dilip Kumar was a highly emotional and technically brilliant film actor when it came to sad and serious roles, the Nargis-Raj Kapoor films, due to their extraordinary common chemistry, made, on average, more money than the Dilip Kumar starrer movies did.

Raj Kapoor's Stubborn Persistence with Film-Making Continued Unabated

Raj Kapoor, true to the characteristics of his gender, did not share the same responsibilities as Nargis after marriage. Thus, although badly hurt by his breakup with Nargis, he most stubbornly persisted with his film career. However, barring his appearance in *Anari* (1959) opposite Nutan, which saw glimpses of the good old Raj Kapoor, his acting also suffered. He had started looking out-of-shape. To be admired by the cinema-goers of India, Indian heroes need to look fit—much like Salman Khan, Aamir Khan, Shahrukh Khan, Hrithik Roshan, Saif Ali Khan, Akshay Kumar, and others. Raj Kapoor, though, had dragged himself too long in the film industry, even when he began to look out of shape.

Prizes do come to those who do not quit. He got his big success with the release of the 1960 blockbuster film *Jis Desh Mein Ganga Behti Hai*, which fetched him India's most coveted Filmfare Award. Earlier, in 1959, he had acted in *Do Ustad* too, which was expected to do well, but it flopped, and its producer, Sheikh Mukhtar, left permanently for Pakistan thereafter. Then, he acted in another lacklustre film, *Chhalia,* in 1960. *Dil Hi To Hai,* made in 1963, was a fiscal success. Raj Kapoor, though not at his best in later years, proved to be a stubborn filmmaker and actor. In the meanwhile, he kept inspiring all the younger Kapoors to remain in the film industry.

Amitabh Bachchan: The Octogenarian Who Is Going Strong

Most of us have seen the very popular television show *Kaun Banega Crorepati.* It is hosted by Amitabh Bachchan. This proves that in the film industry of Mumbai, at present, we have one larger-than-life superstar in Amitabh Bachchan, who is the son of the famous Hindi poet Harivansh Rai Bachchan of Uttar Pradesh. Their ancestors were from Punjab. Amitabh Bachchan's most productive years passed long ago, but due to his undiminishing hunger for work, he is still in demand. Several top-notch female actors have been paired with him, and they all have gained a lot from his name and fame, but none of them became his permanent favourite partner. Compared to the fine lineup of his female opposites in his films, he ended up marrying a short and petite but overall brilliant actor, Jaya Bhaduri, now Jaya Bachchan. She is now a popular politician in India's political circles. At present, she is a member of the Indian Parliament.

Amitabh Bachchan has an impressive and heavy male voice suited for speaking Allahabadi Urdu and Indo-Gangetic Hindustani *lingua franca.* Although his mother, Teji Bachchan, was a typical Punjabi lady, his own Punjabi is severely faulty, but his control over the Hindi language is amazing. He is still lending his voice to many high-end commercials both in the private and public sectors. After the recent demise of the oldest superstar of the Indian film industry, Dilip Kumar, Amitabh Bachchan is now one of the last of the old guards who is still in play.

Cinema-goers of Amitabh Bachchan's age group are his ardent admirers, though in the years gone by, they liked his contemporaries too. When it comes to the amount of work, he only takes on what he can physically handle. Being the grand old man of present-day Indian cinema, Amitabh Bachchan gets a lot of government-sponsored advertisements, too. He also promotes several world-class corporate giants of India. At the tremendously popular beating retreat ceremony that happens daily at the Attari-Wagah border in Amritsar, his voice introduces the history of our Border Security Force. It is a ten-minute-long introduction to the Border Security Force of India and is very popular with tourists. He has appeared in several nationally important commercials, too, including those involving serious ailments like TB (Tuberculosis). Amitabh Bachchan enjoys reasonably good health. He is the patriarchal head of his family. His son, Abhishek Bachchan, an actor, and his celebrity wife and former Miss World – a beauty queen, model, and actor – Aishwarya Rai Bachchan, live with him in his house.

Excitement Amongst Pakistanis to Watch the Great Indian Movies

Once, when Amritsar Doordarshan (DD) was scheduled to screen Meena Kumari's blockbuster film *Paqeeza* (1972), an order came from Islamabad to make a complete recording of this film in the Lahore studio of Pakistan Television Service. The gentry of Lahore was present in the studio where the recording was to be done. This recording was made available in Islamabad, where it was screened for the political and military elite of

Pakistan. Maybe something similar was enacted in Karachi as well. This is just one such example of how Pakistan had gone all out to see India's best films.

Pakistan's terrestrial TV is still in the old analogue system, although Indian Doordarshan has completely switched over to the digital format. DD Amritsar had analogue terrestrial transmitters, and the Pakistani viewers were watching Amritsar DD with old-fashioned rooftop antennae. In 2021, the then-CEO of Prasar Bharati ordered the closure of DD Amritsar by 31 December 2021. For the sake of Pakistani audiences, I requested him to keep the analogue transmitters alive till such a time when Pakistan, too, could go digital, but he closed the analogue transmissions from Amritsar. As a result, Pakistani viewers who are computer illiterate and have no access to smartphones cannot watch even the news that is aired here in India.

Filmography

Andaz (1949)

Nargis was cast against both top-of-the-line actors Dilip Kumar and Raj Kapoor in 1949 in *Andaz*. This role tested her faculties to the hilt. After that, in both *Hulchul* (1951) and *Deedar* (1951), she was again cast opposite Dilip Kumar. These were probably the last films of Nargis and Dilip Kumar being portrayed together. Perhaps *Andaz* indicated things to expect in future. After superb roles of both Dilip Kumar and Raj Kapoor in *Andaz*, Raj Kapoor emerged as the favourite male star opposite Nargis. In this film, Nargis was completely at ease in Western clothes—breaches and pants. She played the role of an emancipated young lady, more like a European freewheeling lady, spoiled by the deep pockets of her father. Her role in this film was markedly domineering than the roles of both Dilip Kumar and Raj Kapoor. Her acting was way ahead of her time, and it would not be wrong to say that she was the fulcrum of the film. Naushad composed outstanding music for the landmark movie. Two songs sung by Lata Mangeshkar for Nargis sealed her permanent slot in movies—*Uthaye Ja Unke Sitam* and *Tod Diya Dil Mera*. These were landmark sad songs.

Nargis also took the daring step of shooting Dilip Kumar's character dead on screen in this one-of-a-kind film. The dancing queen of the film was Kukku, the predecessor of Helen. As usual, she performed at her best.

Lessons Learnt from Aah (1953)

Raj Kapoor took a lot of risks when he dared to make a tragic film like *Aah* in 1953. Perhaps he believed that Nargis' acting could make up for the hero's death at the end of the film and that she would be able to prevent it from falling into the jaws of commercial death just by her prowess. It flopped at the box office as it showed the hero dying of tuberculosis at the end. Indian cinema-goers did not take the death of the hero kindly, especially the one hero that they admired the most. It would not be wrong to conclude that some of the cinema-goers developed a lot of sympathy with Nargis. They could not tolerate the heartbreak of their favourite female actor. The highly emotional lovers of cinema idols worshipped them. As a side note, did you know that when the great Tamil actor M. G. Ramachandran died, a lot of his fans committed suicide?

Everything aside, the music of *Aah* was a smashing success. So much so that later on, as time passed, its superb music pulled it from the brink of a fiscal catastrophe. This film provided excellent entertainment up to its halfway mark, but the moment Raj Kapoor was diagnosed with the dreaded disease, tuberculosis, the interest of the film audience took a nose dive. It was the superb music of the film that took it out of the mounting losses. In addition, the couple made money by acting in non-R. K. films like *Anhonee* (1952) and *Bewafa* (1952). *Aah* taught Raj Kapoor many lessons and made him wiser for his later films. The emotional and sad music of *Raja Ki Aayegi Baraat* was liked by many. Its alaap is mesmerising, and its recording was perfect. Another beauty from this film was the Mukesh-Lata Mangeshkar duet, *Aaja Re Ab Mera Dil Pukara*. It was melodious to the core. Other great songs of the movie – *Yeh Shaam Ki Tanhaiyan* and *Jo Main Janti Unke Liye* – were both in the voice of Lata Mangeshkar. Every one of its songs was a real beauty. Another Mukesh number, *Raat Andheri Door Savera*, was also a great melody. Another lesser-known Lata Mangeshkar-Mukesh duet, *Jane Na Nazar*, was a song that was high on romance melody.

During the same year, in 1953, Shanker-Jaikishan, along with *Aah*, composed music for several other great musicals like *Aas*, *Aurat*, *Naya Ghar*, *Patita*, and *Shikast*. Each song in these films served as a guide for the other movies.

I noticed that the first radio station to play the songs of *Aah* was Radio Ceylon, Colombo, which played all its songs on the eve of the release of the film in an exclusive half-hour slot. The channels that followed shortly afterwards were Radio Pakistan's two important stations in Karachi and Lahore. Surprisingly, All India Radio broadcasted *Aah*'s music for the first time in 1957 when the Vividh Bharati service was produced in the studios of

All India Radio (AIR) Bombay and was relayed on short-wave by AIR Bombay and Madras when it started. The same happened to the music of *Shree 420* in 1955 and to *Chori Chori* in 1956. Radio Ceylon and Radio Pakistan can safely claim to be the first and second to broadcast the music of these great musicals.

Shree 420 (1955)

Raj Kapoor's next venture was *Shree 420,* made in 1955, a film with a strong social theme, which was a huge hit. Its most romantic duet, *Pyar Hua Iqrar Hua,* is its most beautiful and long surviving song, choreographed and picturised as beautifully as it was composed. In the song, *Ramaiya Vastavaiya,* too, Nargis acted as a lady who was thoroughly devoted to her love. It became popular in the year of its release and is still maintaining its popularity well into the twenty-first century. Most people do not understand the meaning of its opening words, but still, they like it. That is the beauty of its great music. This song is still played by disc jockeys at various parties for middle-aged and senior citizen groups in Mumbai and other major cities of India. My personal liking is for Lata Mangeshkar's sad solo number, *O Janewale.* There is also an off-the-beaten-track chorus song, *Mud Mud Ke Na Dekh,* which has its roots in the Western music of London, Los Angeles, and the Broadway of Manhattan in New York City. By the time of this song's release, Raj Kapoor had established himself as the leading showman of Indian cinema. In acting and histrionic skills, however, Dilip Kumar was no less.

In *Shree 420,* Raj Kapoor is shown as a village dude who, in the beginning, is both simple and stupid. However, on reaching Mumbai, he quickly masters the tricks of cheating and treachery to make a quick buck. At one point in the film, he amasses plenty of wealth and learns to rub shoulders with the rich and powerful of the city. On the other hand, the heroine, Nargis, is portrayed as a virtuous, pious lady who is financially very weak, but she is against amassing ill-gotten wealth by using foul means. She wants Raj Kapoor to shun pilferage and cheating and become a law-abiding gentleman. The music of the film was influenced by the music of another film titled *Seema*, which was another great blockbuster of the same year. It is tough to say which of the two films has better music.

Shree 420 showcases the vulgar show of wealth in an incident where the rich elite of Mumbai are gambling at the time of Diwali—just like it happened in the pre-partition days in Punjab's largest and most well-off cities of Lahore and Amritsar. Millions of rupees were gambled in the two cities without the fear of police intervention. After 1947, Lahore, after its demographic change, had become a Muslim city and, perhaps, gotten rid of the scourge of Diwali-eve gambling. But it still happened in Amritsar, though on a much smaller scale. Lahore's highly pampered, wealthy Hindu elite, who had to leave their homes and businesses in 1947, had thinly spread themselves in Delhi, Amritsar, Lucknow, Kanpur, Allahabad, Jaipur, Chandigarh, Mumbai, and Kolkata, to name a few cities. Raj Kapoor brilliantly portrayed the pomp and show of glamour of the Diwali-eve gambling on a massive scale in a song sequence that lasted for less than five minutes—*Mud Mud Ke Na Dekh*. The song was, most tastefully, shot with the leading star Nadira in a palatial British-style building in Mumbai. On one side, there were wild scenes of boundless enjoyment and vulgar show of wealth, and on the other side, Nargis was shown sulking at the humiliation that she suffered at the hands of the power-drunk rich. She was paying the price of her lofty principles of honest and virtuous living.

Raat aur Din (1967): The Great Musical

After remaining cut off from the film industry for a long time, Nargis agreed to act in *Raat Aur Din* in 1967. Along the lines of her 1950s films, this film was also a great musical. Once again, the music of Shanker and Jaikishan was made the centrepiece of the film. The playback voice was again that of Lata Mangeshkar. *Dil Ki Girah Khol Do, Aawara Ae Mere Dil,* and *Jeena Humko Raas Na Aaya* are worth mentioning. Most of the Nargis era's contemporary film-goers showed up at the cinema halls to see their favourite actor once again. I was one of those. By that time, Nargis, though a great actor, was well past her prime age. Perhaps her health was also not at its best. This film did not do that well at the box office. It gave an unambiguous indication to her that maybe her time to say goodbye to films was near. She devoted the rest of her life to social causes and went on to become a parliamentarian, too.

Ek Dil Aur Sao Afsane (1963): Raj Kapoor After the Break Up

For the first time, after so many years of separation from Nargis, Raj Kapoor appeared to be perfectly at ease with another seasoned female actor—Waheeda Rehman—in the 1963 released film *Ek Dil Sao Afsane*. This film did remarkably well at the box office. Before that, he seemed quite at home in *Anari* (1959) as well. The music of both was composed by the tried and tested duo of Shanker and Jaikishan, who were still outstanding. The complete harmony between Raj Kapoor and Waheeda Rehman can be seen in the song *Sunoji Suno Hamari Bhi Suno*.

Sangam, made in 1964, starring Raj Kapoor, Vyjayanthimala, and Rajinder Kumar, was a reasonably well-made movie. Although it was a conventional love triangle musical, it had a fresh appeal. In this film, veteran actor-dancer Vyjayanthimala outshone both the top showman, Raj Kapoor and jubilee celebrator actor, Rajinder Kumar. While the latter part of the South Indian dancing queen's career wasn't as brilliant as her earlier stint, this turned out to be a stellar performance. As usual, the music composed by Shanker and Jaikishan was up to the mark.

Mera Naam Joker, made in 1970, was a high-budget film based on Raj Kapoor's own life story, but it flopped at the box office. It gave a huge financial and psychological setback to the actor, and for a moment, it put a break on his future ambitions. His reputation as a commercially successful producer took a big hit. Raj Kapoor made *Kal Aaj Aur Kal* in 1971, featuring his father, himself, and his son. It was in this movie that he launched his elder son, Randhir Kapoor. Normally, film personalities get Padma Shri as their first national Padma Award, but due to Raj

Kapoor's big name and fame as a showman, he received Padma Vibhushan in 1971.

Bobby (1973): An Attempt to Recreate the Best Years With Nargis

After trying several permutations and combinations with younger actors like Sadhna, Raj Shree, and Hema Malini, Raj Kapoor could not repeat the pleasure of success that he used to enjoy after the release of his earlier films like *Aag* (1948), *Barsaat* (1949), *Bewafa* (1952), *Awaara* (1951), *Aah* (1953), *Shri 420* (1955), and *Chori Chori* (1956). Even the great actor and dancer Vyjayanthimala could not give him the satisfaction that he was looking for. This is despite the scandal with the South India star that was reported by some of the tabloids. In his imagination, he decided to grow young. In his dreams, he wanted to project his younger son as an embodiment of himself during the days of his pairing with Nargis. What he could not do in the company of his favourite star, Nargis, he allowed his son, Rishi Kapoor, and the heroine opposite him, Dimple Kapadia, to do. One of my friends, a frequent movie-goer, after seeing *Bobby*, called it a movie of unlimited hugs. The unprecedented success of this movie prompted other filmmakers to adopt the successful formula of unlimited hugs and kisses, and one of the most successful post-*Bobby* films was *Julie* (1975). *Bobby*, the most successful film of 1973, benefitted its heroine Dimple Kapadia immensely, who later became a highly successful actor and played some of the most glamorous roles. One of my friends said, 'If you have tonnes of money and you are a bachelor, the ideal lady to fall in love with is Dimple Kapadia!' Dimple probably knew the possibility of such incidents. So, she decided to marry when she was less than 20.

Bobby was a typical love story shot partly in Swiss-type locations in Kashmir. In this film, Raj Kapoor discovered the voice of playback singer Shailendra Singh and also brought in a famous Bhajan singer, Narinder Chanchal, from Amritsar. He also discovered Raj Kavi Inderjit Singh Tulsi for composing the lyrics. This film ran to packed houses and recovered all the losses of *Mera Naam Joker* (1970). Later, *Mera Naam Joker* (1970) also rebounded and attained the status of a cult movie, which is being curiously exhibited even to this day.

Raj Kapoor made another average film, *Dharam Karam* (1975), without much success. Being a typical Punjabi, he was very stubborn as a filmmaker. He did not abandon his profession of film-making even when his health appeared to be deteriorating. Even when Raj Kapoor was a shattered man, he remained an iron-willed person who persisted in his profession.

A Reassured Raj Kapoor's Return to Films

Flying on the wings of his impeccable reputation, at one time, Raj Kapoor was toying with the task of building the career of

several young beauties in Mumbai's film industry. Hailing from the modern IT (Information Technology) city of Hyderabad Deccan, Zeenat Aman was a modern emancipated woman. She was born in 1951 and was at least a generation younger than Raj Kapoor. She went to elite schools, which built her one-of-a-kind personality too. In 1970, she appeared in a beauty contest and won the Miss India Earth title. Raj Kapoor was attracted towards her. Perhaps he saw the making of another Nargis in her. He showed interest in building her career as a model and an actor. He was not alone; several veteran actors like Dev Anand were also infatuated with her persona. Raj Kapoor wanted to feature her in his films, and thus, she went on to star in his *Satyam Shivam Sundaram* (1978) as a charming young lady with an accidentally burnt face on one side. The film received critical appreciation from the film-goers in all the regions of India. In the movie, Raj Kapoor created such an illusion that despite looking very badly disfigured on one side of her visage, she was still a ravishing beauty on the other side. Dev Anand went a step further. In his film *Hare Rama Hare Krishna* (1971), he depicted Zeenat Aman as a freewheeling girl who smoked and drank at will and was unafraid of the conservatism of the society around her. Similarly, Raj Kapoor wanted to project another young beauty, Padmini Kohlapuri.

Raj Kapoor's health started deteriorating slowly, but his zeal to keep producing more movies persisted unabated. He worked with several young female actors. Some were moderately successful, but some failed miserably.

By this stage, Raj Kapoor had built his exclusive fan base, something that was independent of the long-ago-separated Nargis-Raj Kapoor base. None of his faithful followers missed visiting the nearest cinema hall where his latest movie used to be screened, with the hope that his new film would be a runaway hit just like the films of the Nargis-Raj Kapoor era.

I am not a mind reader, but I can possibly understand why Raj Kapoor started drinking excessively. Overall, he had a highly successful career as a filmmaker, and financially, he was under pressure only for short durations of time as he bounced back soon after a money-losing venture. When the video cassette recorders were at the peak of their popularity, he would get a print made of one of his vintage films and start watching it from beginning to end. His favourite films were the ones from the earliest part of his life, which were, more often than not, in the esteemed company of Nargis. He often watched evergreen films like *Humayun* (1945), *Mela* (1948), *Aag* (1948), *Anokha Pyar* (1948), *Anhonee* (1952), *Bewafa* (1952), *Andaz* (1949), *Barsaat* (1949), *Awaara* (1951), *Aah* (1953), *Shree 420* (1955), *Boot Polish* (1954), and *Chori Chori* (1956). Some of his non-Nargis favourite films were *Anari* (1959), *Jis Desh Main Ganga Behti Hai* (1960), *Sangam* (1964), *Kal Aaj Aur Kal* (1971), *Mera Naam Joker* (1970), *Satyam Shivam Sundaram* (1978), and *Bobby* (1973).

At one time, Raj Kapoor started consuming a lot more liquor than his body could handle. Although he acted in several movies, his finest career as an actor was all but over. *Jis Desh Main Ganga Behti Hai*, made in 1960, was a well-made film, but he looked out of shape. Despite this, it won several coveted awards, including the most sought-after Filmfare Award for the best film of the year. Such was this man's charisma!

Nargis: The Busy Housewife and Mother

Nargis wanted to be a perfect housewife and the most caring mother for her three kids; the eldest, a boy—Sanjay Dutt—

received more attention than the other two. She desired to see him as a successful film actor. His first movie, *Rocky*, was ready for release on 8 May 1981. Nargis wanted to see it and then critically analyse it, but fate did not permit it to happen. Her health started deteriorating rapidly. When Nargis was diagnosed with pancreatic cancer, her husband, Sunil Dutt, arranged the best medical treatment that he could afford. She was treated at the elite hospitals of Mumbai and in New York. In New York, she was admitted into The Memorial Sloan Kettering Cancer Centre, where, at one stage, she went into a deep coma. Many times, the expert doctors in the hospital concluded that the coma was irreversible. They advised the family to pull the plug on the life support system, but Sunil Dutt loved Nargis too much to do that. To his immense pleasure, she came out of the coma, but her condition deteriorated again after a few days. She was taken back to Mumbai, where, despite the best possible care, she could not be saved, and died at the young age of 52 due to complications related to the spread of cancer on 3 May 1981 in Breach Candy Hospital, Mumbai. Had Nargis been hale and hearty, she would have seen *Rocky* (1981) and, after observing Sanjay Dutt's superb acting, would have been proud of him. The person that she was, though, she would have also corrected his faulty accent in the Hindustani language.

Nargis, born on 1 January 1929 in Kolkata, lived in this world only for 52 years, but through her excellent performances in all the films she starred in, she left wonderful memories behind. Her death was mourned all over India and Pakistan. Radio Ceylon (Sri Lanka Broadcasting Corporation (SLBC) Hindi Service) paid glowing tributes to her in their 7.30 a.m. to 8 a.m. daily show of vintage film music and several other shows year after year. All India Radio's immensely popular Vividh Bharati service, based in Mumbai, also presented some highly emotional programmes in her memory. Songs picturised on her are still being played over the radio years after her death.

Nargis was buried with due state honours in the Bara Kabristan. Some of the mourners in the funeral procession were seen sobbing.

She had a very short, decade-long stint in the film industry. During that period, Nargis had established complete dominance in the industry. Then, she took a U-turn to become a housewife and a mother, which she did as well as possible in a short span before getting stricken by cancer. The only other lady capable of challenging her supremacy was Madhubala, who also had a severe medical problem, which was incurable during those days, and her career was cut short at the young age of 36 in 1969. Meena Kumari was another great actor who had severe medical problems, which cut short her life as well. The only lady, in recent times, who has been able to match the talent of Nargis is Madhuri Dixit. She is pretty, a good orator, and a great classical dancer. Thankfully, she does not suffer from any serious ailment. After getting married, Madhuri Dixit bade a temporary farewell to the film industry, but after her kids started taking care of themselves on their own, she came back to Mumbai. Now, she is back in her profession. The years that she spent in America after her marriage have hurt her professionally, but she is enjoying the small roles that she is getting these days. Maybe we will see more of her sometime soon. Hope keeps cine-goers alive!

India's most famous writer, Khushwant Singh, was fond of the country's finest actors like Nargis, Madhubala, Meena Kumari, and several others. Sunil Dutt, who was from northern India, was fond of travelling to the beautiful hill stations of Uttarakhand and Himachal Pradesh. One day, both he and

Nargis were in the Simla-Kasauli area. All the decent hotels in the area were fully booked. Khushwant Singh had a beautifully kept cottage in Kasauli. On someone's advice, Nargis called up Khushwant Singh to seek his permission to stay in his cottage. He picked up the phone, and after confirming that she was the real Nargis Dutt, he told her that it would be his pleasure to host the couple, but there was one condition—they would have to sleep in his bedroom. The couple promised to do so and stayed there in perfect five-star comfort. Later, Khushwant Singh bragged about it several times. This story is still very popular in Kasauli.

Raj Kapoor and the Sikh Community

Raj Kapoor's forefathers were gurdwara-going Hindus in the North West Frontier Province. Raj Kapoor's father, Prithvi Raj Kapoor, was born in the town of Samundri, which had a significant Sikh population with an army background. Later, while living in Mumbai, his father used to go to a local gurdwara regularly. Although Raj Kapoor was born in the Pathan city of Peshawar, his schooling took place in an English medium secondary school in the United Provinces. Raj Kapoor was never exposed to the crude Talbanistic system of the North West Frontier Province.

Raj Kapoor's younger brother, Shammi Kapoor, was married to a Sikh girl, Harkirtan Kaur (Geeta Bali), the daughter of a Sikh preacher and philosopher, Pandit Kartar Singh of Amritsar. Raj Kapoor's father, Prithvi Raj Kapoor, preferred Sikh rites during births, deaths, and weddings in the family. For instance, his granddaughter, Karishma Kapoor, was married to a family of Sikh industrialists in New Delhi. Her *anand karaj* was performed by Bhai Harbans Singh of Jagadhri and his party, then settled in Ludhiana. Raj Kapoor's parentage could be called half Sikh.

The city of New York's Asian-Indian population during the mid-1980s was approximately 60 per cent Gujarati, 20 per cent Punjabi Sikhs, and the rest were from all the remaining states of India. The rush of computer technocrats from Bengaluru and Hyderabad in southern India had not invaded America yet.

Every year, New York celebrates the India Day Parade on the first Saturday or Sunday after the Independence Day of India. At the time, most of the participants were Gujaratis. Some wealthy Sikhs, especially from Manhattan and Long Island areas of New York, also used to take part in the parade. Events related to Operation Blue Star (June 1984) in the Golden Temple deeply hurt every Sikh's psyche. The events that occurred in November of 1984, after the assassination of the then Prime Minister, Mrs Indira Gandhi, made matters worse. The angry Sikhs made up their mind to start their own Sikh Day Parade after the Festival of Baisakhi in April, on the last Saturday of the month.

Around 1986–87, Raj Kapoor was invited to become the grand marshal of the India Day Parade. He was not aware of the psychological impact of Operation Blue Star that had occurred in June of 1984. Although the Indian Government tried to keep a tight lid on the happenings inside the Golden Temple, the BBC (British Broadcasting Corporation) London's chief reporter in India, Mark Tully, was clandestinely staying in Amritsar and sending out news dispatches. The American media, such as the Columbia Broadcasting System (CBS) News, National Broadcasting Company (NBC) News, NPR News, and ABC News, were also carrying the news of the operation. Every news was getting to the Sikhs through the American, British, and Canadian media. The Sikh community was full of anguish. Spontaneous protests by the Sikh diaspora erupted in most major cities abroad. New York City saw the biggest demonstrations on the East Coast of America. On the India Day Parade, which was in the third week of August, many Sikhs demonstrated against the action of the Central Government of India (equivalent to America's Federal Government) in 1986 and 1987 as well.

An innocent showman, Raj Kapoor, got caught between these protesters and the organisers of the parade. The Consulate General of India, since the inception of the parade, was the driving force behind this annual event. Wherever Raj Kapoor went, there were some Sikhs already present. Being unfamiliar with such ticklish situations, Raj Kapoor turned out to be the most confused grand marshal of the India Day Parade! The pure, poor soul could not distinguish between a protester and a participant in the parade. For a person with fast-deteriorating health, those were the scariest moments in his life. He was facing protests from a community which he and his father always called his own. Soon after the parade was over, he abruptly left for India. In India, his health took a turn for the worse, and to bear it, he began drinking beyond his capacity.

Raj Kapoor's Death

Although he preferred to hide the fact that he missed Nargis and was happy in the presence of all the other younger actors all through his youthful days, in his later years, when his overall level of energy went down, his habit of drinking too heavily at unusual hours pointed clearly to the fact that he was seriously in love with Nargis, and what he had been showing thus far had all been a lie. He ached for Nargis, and that was the only truth.

Film duplication technology was advancing very fast. Video Cassette Recorders (VCRs) had invaded the market and made duplicating films a much easier task. He got copies of all his films with Nargis. He used to watch one film in one sitting. Side by side, he kept drinking liquor. His habit of excessive drinking got exacerbated as time passed, and his health kept deteriorating. He started looking aged, rundown, and depressed. Nargis had left the world a few years earlier. To be candid, Raj Kapoor had also made up his mind to leave this world.

In recognition of Raj Kapoor's lifelong service to India's film industry, the Government of India decided to confer the highest award in the film industry, known as the Dada Sahib Phalke Award for the year 1987, on Raj Kapoor. This was sort of a lifetime achievement award for India's biggest-ever showman. The government knew that his habit of drinking excessively was not going to be reversed. Some people assert that he used to cry in solitude. However, no one can confirm the authenticity of this information. When the coveted award was about to be handed over, his health deteriorated even further. The award was handed over to him in a jiffy, and he was rushed to the top hospital, but he never fully recovered from his chronic health problems. His death came on 2 June 1988.

In addition to India, his loss was mourned by the folks of movie-going intelligentsia all over the world, including all of India's neighbouring countries in the southern and southeast Asian regions. The major national news bulletins of All India Radio, in both English and Hindi, paid rich tributes to the memory of Raj Kapoor. Radio Ceylon (Hindi Service of Sri Lanka Broadcasting Corporation Colombo) and Vividh Bharati service of All India Radio Bombay presented special exclusive programmes in memory of Raj Kapoor. The Urdu External

Service of All India Radio beamed to Pakistan had also paid glowing tributes to his fond memory. Most of the capital stations of All India Radio, including India's flagship station in New Delhi and All India Radio stations at Lucknow, Patna, Bhopal, Raipur, Jaipur, and Jalandhar, paid special tributes to him. Similarly, the Doordarshan stations in New Delhi, Lucknow, Patna, Bhopal, and Jalandhar carried special audio-visual programmes on his life and times. His movies are still being screened at Prasar Bharati Corporation's Doordarshan stations spread over the length and breadth of India. It has been many years since Raj Kapoor passed away, but his memories are immortal. Songs from his movies are still being played frequently in Sri Lanka Broadcasting Corporation's programme on the *Purani Filmon Ka Sangeet* programme every morning from 7.30 a.m. to 8 a.m. and on Vividh Bharati's programme *Bhoole Bisre Geet,* which precedes the SLBC programme, from 7 a.m. to 7.30 a.m. every morning.

After his death, his loving sons and grandkids are keeping his memories alive. The latest star in the family is his grandson, Ranbir Kapoor, who is doing very well professionally. He is married to one of India's most brilliant actors of recent times—Alia Bhatt.

As an afterthought, I believe Nargis and Raj Kapoor, even after years of separation, used to consider themselves a part of each other's life. Raj Kapoor was a great thinker; he had fantastic ideas, but Nargis had the unique professional capability to transform those ideas into reality. During her most creative days, although Madhubala was by far the most beautiful female actor, Nargis had no equal in acting capabilities. Madhubala's health problem was detected around the *Mughal-e-Azam* era. After that, her health deteriorated quite quickly. Her best period ended before the release of *Mughal-e-Azam*. Meena Kumari, Nutan, Vyjayanthimala, and Waheeda Rehman have been great female actors and very good dancers as well. Nargis was not a great dancer, but she compensated for this drawback with her superb acting talent. Being the daughter of a classical musician, she perfectly knew what a *taal* meant, and she acted perfectly in *taal* to every song.

Whenever needed, Nargis and Raj Kapoor sincerely helped each other. Throughout their time as the hero and heroine, they were selfless. When it came to direction, no other music director could match the success rate of Shanker and Jaikishan for the Nargis and Raj Kapoor combination. Only two films under the other music directors did better at the box office and nationwide record sales. These were *Anarkali* (1953) under the music direction of C. Ramchandra and *Nagin* (1954) under the music direction of Hemant Kumar Mukherjee. Both were admittedly great musicals.

Had Nargis and Raj Kapoor not had a breakup, they would have given many more silver and golden jubilee films to the country. Their unfortunate breakup hurt entire India. Nargis was a perfect teacher of acting to the younger generations. She would have made Raj Kapoor a much better-trained actor but the chain of events precluded it. God wished Sunil Dutt to be a loving husband to a virtuous woman. Despite being a deprived refugee from Pakistani Punjab, he deserved a good, decent bride, and in Nargis, he got the best. In return, Sunil Dutt gave Nargis the respect and adoration that she deserved, and she proved to be not only an ideal wife but an exceptional teacher and a guide, too. The irony is that Nargis had a lifespan that was too short.

When one watches Nargis-Raj Kapoor films, it is evident that it was not only the famous duo of brilliant actors but a well-engineered machine with six parts moving in perfect synchronisation. The other four parts were music directors Shanker and Jaikishan and poets (lyricists) Hasrat Jaipuri and Shailendra. Hasrat Jaipuri was the oldest member of the team and the longest to survive. He was born on 14 April 1922, and he died on 17 September 1999 at the age of 77. Shanker was born on 15 October 1922 and died on 26 April 1987 at the age of 64. Shailendra was born on 30 August 1923 and was the second youngest to die on 14 December 1966 at age 43. Jaikishan was the youngest to be born on 4 November 1929 and the youngest to die on 12 September 1971 at the age of 42. This team included one more person to whom no one gives any credit. He was the assistant music director, Dutta Ram, who was a great percussionist. They are all gone now, but their music still lingers.

In the modern generation, most would not have seen their films and, hence, would not know how great of a professional each one of them was. The new generation of movie-goers should watch their films and listen to their songs, all of which are now available on YouTube. By listening to the music of their films, the younger generation will get to know how lovely and melodious the songs were and how entertaining their films were.

For the past several years, I have been a member of a popular Facebook group devoted to the music of Shanker and Jaikishan. The name of the group is *Shanker-Jaikishan: Maestros of the Millennium*. The main force behind this group is an America-based professional lady, Lakhmi K. Tummala, who is a no-nonsense and highly committed administrator of the group. This group is still very vibrant, the members of which share a lot of information about the greatness of Shanker and Jaikishan.

There was an attempt to deliberately avoid the inclusion of the playback singers Mukesh and Manna Dey for Raj Kapoor and Lata Mangeshkar for Nargis in the overall team of Nargis-Raj Kapoor, but without them, the name and fame attained by the brand Nargis and Raj Kapoor would not have been possible.

Before the Internet age, I had tried to collect the records of Shanker and Jaikishan's best music. During the golden period of gramophones, my late father, Sardar Sochet Singh, started collecting 78 RPM records as far back as 1932. I kept his hobby alive by adding more gramophone records of the finest music directors, which include, among others, the unforgettable music of Pandit Amar Nath, Master Ghulam Haider, Anil Biswas, C. Ramchandra, Sajjad Hussain, Khem Chand Prakash, Naushad, Shyam Sunder, Madan Mohan, Husan Lal, Bhagat Ram, Sachin Dev Burman, Jaidev, Vinod, Hans Raj Behl, Sardul Singh Kwatra, S. Mohinder, and Shanker-Jaikishan. The music of Nargis-Raj Kapoor and Shanker-Jaikishan combination owes a lot to Radio Ceylon (SLBC), primarily its great producers and disc jockeys such as Gopal Sharma, Vijay Kishore Dubey, Ameen Sayani, Manohar Mahajan, Vijay Luxmi, and Dalbir Singh Parmar on short-wave, All India Radio (especially the Urdu and Vividh Bharati Services on short-wave and medium-wave and now FM only), Radio Pakistan (Karachi on short-wave and medium-wave and Lahore on medium-wave), Radio Kabul Urdu Service on short-wave, Radio Iran Zahidan Urdu Service on short-wave, Radio Cairo Urdu Service on short-wave, and the Voice of America Hindi and Urdu Services (through the producers and broadcasters like Vijay Laxmi, Gulshan Madhur, Muazzam Siddiqui, and Mudassira Manzir on short-wave).

The new generation of cinema-goers and listeners of film music of India is, unfortunately, alien to the golden period of film music of India and the golden age of medium-wave and short-wave radio that went hand in hand with the rise of radio and melody. What the younger generation has missed is now available through fast-paced technological innovations. They can enjoy the fine art of movie-making and melody creation of the yore by using modern technological capabilities. There was a time, not long ago, when technology was primitive and India produced its most brilliant music-makers like Shanker and Jaikishan for the Nargis and Raj Kapoor films made between 1948 and 1956. Their finest work is now available, almost in its entirety, through YouTube and other modern technological means. Just by a click of the mouse, all priceless music can be accessed and heard. To improve the quality of music on the computer, an additional amplifier and a couple of high-powered speakers as attachments are necessary. Though all of the members constituting the Nargis-Raj Kapoor extended team are long gone, their work luckily survives to this date and will live as long as human beings are alive on Earth.

Guzra hua zamana aata nahin dobara,
haafiz khuda tumhara…

Music: The Biggest Asset of Raj Kapoor's Films

The quality of music composed by Shanker and Jaikishan played a big role in the runaway success of almost all the Nargis-Raj Kapoor films. Theatre shows of his father's theatre group had reasonably good quality music, but the movies of Nargis and Raj Kapoor, somehow, had exceptionally good music. Raj Kapoor, even in his childhood, was exposed to good quality melodious music. Many a time, it was he who suggested unusual tunes for some of the songs to Shanker and Jaikishan, who brilliantly improvised to create amazing tunes. It is also important to note that Nargis was a self-made choreographer for her dancing items.

On the other hand, her mother, Jaddan Bai (her original childhood name was Fatima Rashid), was a great musician with pan-India recognition. The most famous music directors of those days were Anil Biswas, Khem Chand Prakash, Naushad Ali, and Sajjad Hussain. They were in a special elite league—even the music directors of lesser eminence admired their melodic creativity. Perhaps Raj Kapoor wanted to do something not done by his predecessors and contemporaries. So, he rebelled against all the big names and picked up a brand-new duo of music directors. In 1950, he acted opposite the female superstar of the time—Suraiya, under the music direction of Naushad Ali, but later, he stuck to his discovery of the then lesser-known music directors. The most popular music directors of his time were the duo of Husan Lal and Bhagat Ram, but Raj Kapoor used his fiercely independent judgement in favour of a new and untried duo in Shanker and Jaikishan. During 1949 and 1950, Husan Lal and Bhagat Ram had 20 films in hand for composing music—a record of sorts. It was not easy to pay full attention to the music of such a huge number of films. Raj Kapoor was not afraid of taking risks. The risk he took in choosing Shanker-Jaikishan helped not only the pair of Nargis and Raj Kapoor but numerous other producers as well. Ustad Allah Rakha, the famous tabla player, wanted somebody other than Mukesh to be the playback singer for Raj Kapoor in the film *Bewafa* (1952) – a fact he told me during his 1982–1983 tour of the USA as the tabla player accompanying Pandit Ravi Shankar, the world-famous sitarist. He told me that as the music director of the film, he wanted to use the voice of Mohammad Rafi or Talat Mahmood for Raj Kapoor. After initial hesitation, Raj Kapoor agreed to the voice of Talat Mahmood.

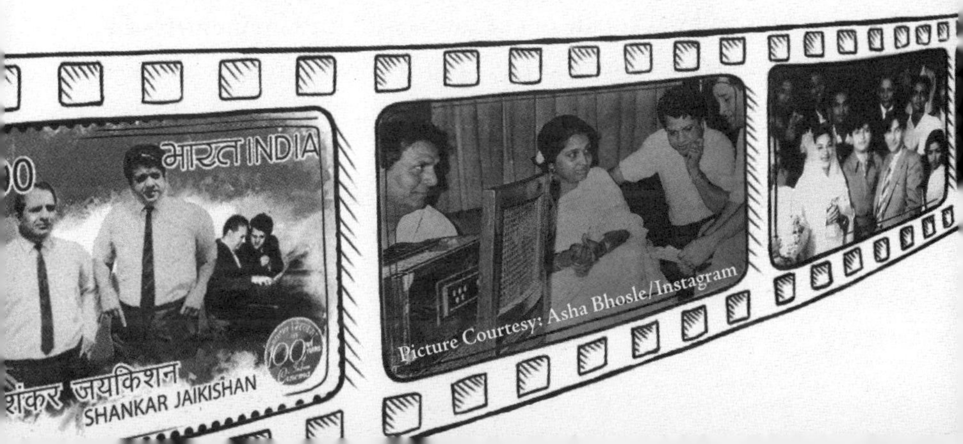

Picture Courtesy: Asha Bhosle/Instagram

Nargis' Strong Approval of Shanker and Jaikishan's Music

Although the sad song *Baharen Phir Bhi Aayengi* from the 1949 film *Lahore*, rendered by Lata Mangeshkar under the music direction of Shyam Sundar, was an early favourite of Nargis, as the songs of the film *Barsaat* (1949) started pouring out, she started liking the music of Shanker-Jaikishan's debut film tremendously. Nargis may not have a direct role in the selection of Shanker and Jaikishan, but she thoroughly enjoyed every take of the songs picturised on her, and as a matter of good fortune, none of these songs flopped. The music directors burnt the midnight oil to compose exceptionally great tunes to be picturised on Nargis. India's ravishing beauty, Madhubala, was another star for whom all the music directors composed their best tunes, and none of the songs flopped. Shanker-Jaikishan worked so hard on each song that none was rejected at the box office by the Indian cinema-goers. Both Nargis and Madhubala gained tremendously from Lata Mangeshkar's brilliant renditions. Although Mohammad Rafi's versatile voice was the choice of most other actors, the support of Mukesh's voice and the songs that were picturised on Raj Kapoor showed that he was the most stubborn when it came to his professional preferences.

During the late 1960s, when Nargis was busy bringing up her kids and was totally out of touch with the film industry, she acted in the film *Raat Aur Din* (1967). Music directors Shanker and Jaikishan were hired again and composed some of their finest numbers for this film.

Shanker and Jaikishan were greenhorns in the profession of film music creation when the Nargis-Raj Kapoor starrer film *Barsaat* (1949) fell into their lap. They showed their unflinching determination to undertake such a huge task. Being the first Nargis-Raj Kapoor film in their kitty, they handled it very professionally and with the utmost confidence. None of its songs could be termed mediocre. They took inspiration from Husan Lal-Bhagat Ram's Punjabi-style melodies, especially the first song, *Hawa Mein Udta Jaaye*. Another great Punjabi-style song was *Mujhe Kisi Se Pyar Ho Gaya*. As time passed, they started using heavy orchestra in their recordings. In the mid-1950s, in some cases, the orchestra consisted of 30–40 violins, two to three tablas, a couple of *dholkis*, and others. In the meanwhile, recording technology was advancing fast, and they used a separate microphone for each of the instruments. The mixing equipment could control each microphone's volume and tonal quality.

The music of the film *Aag* (1948) was reasonably good. It was composed by Ram Ganguli, a meritorious music director, but Raj Kapoor always aspired to set the bar much higher. Luck was on his side. Shanker and Jaikishan did a splendid job. All the songs of *Barsaat* (1949) were to the liking of both Nargis and Raj Kapoor and went on to become hits. The music of his movies was mostly Indian, but there was some sprinkling of Western influence in them as well, which was quite digestible to the average movie-goer. For example, the Mukesh-Lata Mangeshkar duet *Chhod Gaye Balam Mujhe* had a very sweet Western-inspired prelude with the violin as the dominating instrument. It was the sweetest part of the melody. Such preludes and interludes were repeated later in Nargis-Raj Kapoor starrer movies and the productions of several other producers. Both the chosen poets were new, but they wrote like veterans of lyric writing.

As a subject of research as to who could be the best voice for Nargis, Raj Kapoor most probably studied three films in which Nargis was the leading actress. These were *Mela* (1948), *Aag* (1948), and *Anokha Pyar* (1948). In both *Mela* (1948) and *Aag* (1948), Shamshad Begum's voice was the playback voice for Nargis. There was nothing wrong with Shamshad Begum's sharp and crisp voice, but the new find in Lata Mangeshkar was a shade sweeter and much more sophisticated. Also, her voice was already in use by most other popular contemporary actors, including the ravishing beauty Madhubala. Both Nargis and Raj Kapoor most probably informally agreed that the playback voice for Nargis would be that of none other than Lata Mangeshkar. Incidentally, the main choice for playback singing for the female actors of the films, where the music was composed by Shanker and Jaikishan, was also Lata Mangeshkar. In some of the movies, all the songs were sung by Lata Mangeshkar, regardless of the number of female actors. This is visible from all songs of the film *Aurat* (1953), based on a biblical story.

For male playback singing, Raj Kapoor preferred the highly romantic voice of Mukesh. Talat Mahmood's sweet, velvety voice was used for only a few films like *Bewafa* (1952) and *Anhonee* (1952). Later, in films like *Shree 420* (1955) and *Chori Chori* (1956), when Mukesh was not at his professional best to sing for Raj Kapoor, as a substitute, Manna Dey's voice was experimented with, and he performed remarkably well. It is strange to observe that, for some reason, the voice of the most versatile playback singer, Mohammad Rafi, never found favour with Raj Kapoor. Of course, Mohammad Rafi sang in Raj Kapoor's films, but as a singer for other characters. Manna Dey, with a vast treasure of classical music behind him, was technically the most sound playback singer, but he was seldom the first choice of the most particular heroes of the Indian film industry like Raj Kapoor.

Tryst with Hasrat Jaipuri

Hasrat Jaipuri used to serve as a bus conductor in BEST (Bombay Electric Supply and Transport) local bus service. Raj Kapoor, like some other film personalities of Mumbai, had no hesitation in travelling in buses. Once, a poem recited in the local bus by Hasrat Jaipuri impressed Raj Kapoor so thoroughly that he hired him instantly to compose the songs for his film *Barsaat* (1949), and a long-lasting relationship began between the poet and the producer.

Shailendra was born in Rawalpindi—a man hailing from UP. Both were innovative poets. Hasrat Jaipuri's lyrics were heavy on Urdu vocabulary, and Shailendra's were rich in conversational Hindi. Both composed hit songs picturised on Nargis and Raj Kapoor. In real life, Hasrat Jaipuri was an extremely jovial human being who could laugh even at himself. Some of the popular songs penned by him like *Ab Raat Guzarne WaliHai* (*Awara*, 1951), *Mohabbat Ki Dastan Aaj Suno* (*Mayur Pankh*, 1954), *Aa Ja Re Ab Mera Dil Pukara* (*Aah*, 1953), *Kahe Ko Der Lagayi Re* (*Daag*, 1952), *Chhod Gaye Balam* and *Ab Mera Kaun Sahara* (*Barsaat*, 1949), and *Aa Sun Le Mere Dil Ki Pukar* (*Aurat*, 1953) went on to become evergreen melodies. Others like *Haaye Mera Dil Legaya Koi* (*Parbat*, 1952) are heart-touching. Some songs from the film *Poonam* (1952) – *Taqdeer Ka Shikwa Kaun Kare* and *Ab Toh Aa Jaao Balam*, written by Hasrat Jaipuri, became very popular. In fact, these two have been the favourite numbers of Radio Pakistan. Hasrat Jaipuri's songs from *Nagina* (1951), including *Kaisi Khushi Ki Hai Raat*, became very popular among the youth. A song from the 1953 film *Aas*, *Zulm ki Nagri Men*, was one of the favourite songs of Radio Pakistan and Radio Ceylon.

Shailendra and Raj Kapoor

Somewhere, Raj Kapoor read the simple but meaningful poetry of a maverick—Punjab-born (brought up in UP) poet, Shailendra. He used to write for downtrodden folks, and Raj Kapoor liked it. But Shailendra was a blunt man. He straight away refused to write for the film industry. Subsequently, though, circumstances compelled him to agree to Raj Kapoor's request.

Once he got going, he composed some of the finest songs for Nargis-Raj Kapoor movies. These include the title song of the film *Barsaat* (1949), *Barsaat Mein Humse Mile* and *Mujhe Kisi Se Pyar Ho Gaya* from the same movie. More masterpieces included *Dum Bhar Jo Udhar Munh Phere (Awaara,* 1951), *Dard-e-Jigar Thahr Zara* (*Aurat,* 1953), *Tu Pyar Ka Sagar Hai* (*Seema,* 1955), and *Yeh Mera Deewanapan Hai* (*Yahudi,* 1958). For *Aah* (1953), he wrote some sad melodies like *Raja Ki Aayegi Baraat, Yeh Shaam Ki Tanhaiyan,* and *Jo Main Janti Unke Liye.* For *Chori Chori* (1956), he was the soul behind the beautiful song *Man Bhavan Ke Ghar.* He wrote one of the most emotional songs for the film *Shikast* (1953), *Badle Rang Jahan Ke.* For *Patita* (1953), he wrote an extremely sad, *Mitti Se Khelte Ho Bar-Bar Kisliye,* and a thoroughly upbeat song, *Kisine Apana Bana Ke Mujhko.* Similarly, for *Seema* (1955), there is *Baat Baat Mein Rootho Na* as opposed to the aforementioned *Tu Pyar Ka Sagar Hai.* There is a lot of merit in the song *Nanhe Munne Bachche Teri Mutthi Mein* for *Boot Polish* (1954). In *Nagina* (1951), *Tune Hai Mere Zakhm-e-Jigar Ko* was another masterpiece. I shall give equal credit to music directors Shanker and Jaikishan for infusing soul into this song, and the rendition by Lata Mangeshkar is what helped it to attain perfection. The entire team of Nargis-Raj Kapoor acted like a well-trained, all-conquering army, and the credit earned by every small link goes to the generals Nargis-Raj Kapoor and then Shanker-Jaikishan.

Although Shanker-Jaikishan never looked beyond lyricists Hasrat Jaipuri and Shailendra, in hindsight, considering the overall success rate of songs composed by Rajinder Krishan for a lot of music directors, I must admit that he would have made the songs of team Nargis-Raj Kapoor a lot more successful.

Mukesh: Raj Kapoor's Favourite Male Playback Voice

Raj Kapoor's favourite playback singer since his first movie, *Mela* (1948), was Mukesh Chand Mathur, popularly known as Mukesh. However, in some movies like *Anhonee* (1952), *Ashiana* (1952), and *Bewafa* (1952), Talat Mahmood was his playback singer. In a few cases, when Mukesh had health problems, even Manna Dey sang as the playback singer for Raj Kapoor. It perplexes me and some music directors to point out that Mohammad Rafi's soft, sweet, and flexible voice, that too from Raj Kapoor's own province of Punjab, never found favour with the top showman of India. Mohammad Rafi gave his voice to Raj Kapoor in only one song, *Main Zindagi Mein Hardam Rota Hi Raha,* from the film *Barsaat* (1949). Sardul Kwatra thought that Mohammad Rafi was the playback voice for most of his contemporary actors. I am sure if Raj Kapoor had ventured into the Punjabi film industry, the voice of Mohammad Rafi would have been used in his films. Raj Kapoor's father was instrumental in the super success of the Punjabi film *Nanak Naam Jahaz Hai* (1969). Raj Kapoor could not get the opportunity to jump on such a chance.

Lata Mangeshkar: The Quickest Sprint to the Top

1949 saw several landmark musical films. In *Mahal (1949)*, after the recording of its most loved song, *Aayega Aayega Aanewala*, Lata Mangeshkar got established on the throne as the queen of playback singing. The album *Ladli* (1949) reinforced Lata Mangeshkar's claim to the coveted title in the Anil Biswas-composed tune for the song, *Tumhare Bulane Ko Jee Chahta Hai*. Shyam Sunder's tunes for *Lahore* (1949), including the song *Baharen Phir Bhi Aayengi*, picturised on Nargis, and *Bazaar*'s (1949) song *Saajan Ki Galiyan Chhod Chale*, proved the unmatched superiority of Lata Mangeshkar. The songs of films *Andaz* (1949), *Dulari* (1949), *Bazaar* (1949), *Patanga* (1949), *Bari Behen* (1949), *Adhi Raat* (1950), *Lachhi* (Punjabi) (1949), *Bhaiya Ji* (Punjabi) (1950), *Meena Bazaar* (1950), *Afsana* (1951), *Ek Thi Larki* (1949), *Hulchul* (1951), *Sangdil* (1952), and *Tarana* (1951) reinforced the claim of Lata Mangeshkar to stardom in playback singing.

At the time of independence, Noor Jehan, Suraiya, and Geeta Roy were the leading film singers. Noor Jehan migrated to Pakistan soon after independence, leaving the field wide open for the remaining two. During the immediate post-independence period, there was a trio of leading female actors in Indian cinema—Suraiya, Madhubala, and Nargis. Suraiya had the distinction of singing her own songs. In the Madhubala-starrer *Singhar* (1949), music director Khurshid Anwar, in a bold step, selected Surinder Kaur as the playback singer for Madhubala. But with the advent of Lata Mangeshkar in later years, such liberty was no longer available to the music composers.

Lata Mangeshkar rose so above all the others that for both Madhubala and Nargis, the only playback singer could be her.

Music director O. P. Nayyar proved to be an exception and attained so much popularity that he could dictate his terms as the one and only music director who substituted Lata Mangeshkar with Shamshad Begum, Geeta Dutt, and Lata Mangeshkar's younger sister, Asha Bhosle. Surprisingly, all the female actors fell in line with O. P. Nayyar's choice. Incidentally, all three leading ladies of Bollywood had chaste Urdu as their plus point. All three ladies who mattered the most in the Indian film industry happened to be very secular Muslims.

Popular Songs of Nargis and Raj Kapoor's Top Films

Made in 1949, *Barsaat,* the second Nargis-Raj Kapoor film, was not technically an exceptional film, but it turned out to be a big financial success—primarily on the strength of its outstanding music. If the Mukesh-Lata duets are rated, *Chhod Gaye Baalam Mujhe* would be their best song. This number has its roots in the late 1940s Hollywood-American music. The string instrument, the violin, is the dominating musical piece in this one-of-a-kind melody. The chorus of *Barsaat Mein Humse Mile Tum* had a powerful beat. The sad numbers of *Barsaat* (1949), rendered by Lata Mangeshkar, such as *Ab Mera Kaun Sahara, Bichhde Hue Pardesi, Jiya Beqarar Hai Chhayee Bahar,* and *Hawa Mein Udta Jaye* were all good. Mohammad Rafi's number, *Main Zindagi Mein Hardam Rota Hi Raha,* was also a good one. It was pictured very professionally. A lot of credit goes to the music director duo of Shanker and Jaikishan for making their first venture such a super success. Nimmi was a brilliant new find, but she had only a small role to play, most of which was a tear-jerker.

Made in 1951, Raj Kapoor's third film, *Awaara,* was decisively better. Its story had a lot more punch in it. Also, its music was as successful as that of *Barsaat* (1949), if not more. *Awaara's* most romantic song, a Mukesh-Lata duet, shot in a boat in the bright moonlight eclipsed by dark clouds, *Dum Bhar Jo Udhar,* is a melody par excellence. In the song, Nargis looks totally devoted to her love for Raj Kapoor. Mukesh's solo, *Awaara Hoon,* was, of course, the choice of the masses. Another Mukesh solo worth mentioning is *Hum Tujhse Mohabbat Kar Ke.* Lata Mangeshkar's sad number, *Ab Raat Guzarne Wali Hai,* can be termed as the most impressive among sad songs. *Ghar Aaya Mera Pardesi* was another very sweet melody rendered in a chorus format. The superb acting of Raj Kapoor in *Awaara* (1951) received so much appreciation abroad that according to the foreign viewers' choice, his role in this film was termed as one of the ten top-most impressive acting performances put up by any actor in the world. Raj Kapoor played the role of a vagabond and a petty criminal thief. He did full justice to his role. Nargis, too, was great as ever. She played the role of a highly confident and well-brought-up girl who goes on to become a brilliant advocate. In the critical scene of Raj Kapoor's trial, she rose to great heights, which left the jury flabbergasted and the cinema audience spellbound.

By the time *Awaara* (1951) was made, Shanker and Jaikishan were well on the road to developing their distinct style of music by coming out of the shadow of Pandit Husan Lal and Bhagat Ram, who were Shanker's mentors. The Punjabi influence on their music was present, but it enhanced the impact of melody, not mar it. In 1951, music directors Shanker and Jaikishan were quite busy—they composed the music for three more movies—*Badal, Kali Ghata,* and *Nagina.* The music of all these movies became very popular. Shanker-Jaikishan learnt from each song that they created and used the archived tunes in later films. There are several short musical compositions in *Awaara* (1951), which became the tunes of complete songs in later films like *Jis Desh Mein Ganga Behti Hai* (1960). All these songs became hits.

Some people liked prolonged, almost impossible fighting scenes in films. It was believed that the longer the fight between the hero and the villain lasts, the more popular the film will be. Much later, this also led to the long fight in the film *Sholay* (1975) being attributed as the reason for its box office success. But Raj Kapoor did not believe in that kind of generalisation. In *Awaara (1951)*, he shot a fight with Jaggu, the villain, played by the famous actor K. N. Singh. The fight lasted less than two minutes, at the end of which the underdog Raj Kapoor kills the villain. The reputation of Raj Kapoor revolves around such episodes of defying the stereotypical notions in the film industry. Generally, the heroines were made to suffer indignities and mental torture in the Indian film industry, but Nargis was spared of all such harrowing experiences in Raj Kapoor's lively films.

Shanker and Jaikishan: Outstanding Music Directors

British rulers had introduced Western notations of music to the Indian learners of Western music, and subsequently, these same notations became applicable to Indian music as well. Jaikishan used to study Western musical notations in his musical compositions, and he applied what he learned from these notations. During those days, under British and Hollywood influence, the size of orchestras was increasing in India, too, much like the New York Philharmonic Orchestra and Los Angeles Symphony Orchestra. Shanker and Jaikishan were known to have the biggest orchestra in Bollywood, and it also helped the Nargis-Raj Kapoor team, as it gave the songs more depth and vibrance. At times, they used as many as 30–50 violins simultaneously, along with three tablas and a *dholak* at every take, while recording special numbers. Himself a brilliant music director, Duttaram was Shanker and Jaikishan's assistant in music direction. Minoo Kartik was their most used sound recordist. Jaikishan was a man who mingled freely with friends and fans during his spare time in the evenings. On the contrary, Shanker was a quiet creator. Both, together, made the ideal team. A leading violinist in Mumbai, Gajanan, was one of the top confidants of these music directors.

Shanker and Jaikishan were highly innovative music-makers. They created several permutations and combinations in background music as well as the introduction of catchy preludes and interludes in song sequences. However, in the choice of playback singer, Lata Mangeshkar was the one and the only never to be compromised with. In fact, in every song, Lata Mangeshkar positively delivered what the music directors desired from her. They had recorded an off-the-beaten-track Western-style duet in the voices of Mukesh and Lata Mangeshkar for *Badal* (1951), *Ae Dil Na Mujhse Chhupa*—picturised on Madhubala and Prem Nath. Such music was to the liking of both Nargis and Raj Kapoor.

On a visit to Mumbai in 1969, I made a special attempt to personally meet music director Jaikishan Panchal at the Gaylord Restaurant in Central Mumbai. On meeting him, he told me that not only the Shanker-Jaikishan team but even Nargis and Raj Kapoor had gained a lot from the excellent music composed by the duo—both sides gained from the other's outstanding performances. Even the poets Hasrat Jaipuri and Shailendra gained immensely from the music of Shanker and Jaikishan. All three pairs were net beneficiaries of the achievements of the other pairs. For a long time, none of these three pairs experienced a break in partnership. Over the years, they became household names. If anything went wrong with Nargis or Raj Kapoor, a wave of sympathy was generated among the cinema-goers. Similarly, if any sort of mishap happened to Shailendra or Hasrat Jaipuri, the cinema-goers felt the pinch. The same was the case with Shanker-Jaikishan. I remember when *Aah* (1953) failed, the grief was written large on the faces of Hasrat Jaipuri and Shailendra, as well as Shanker and Jaikishan. Eventually, though, when the reality of the excellence in music sunk into the psyche of the common man, the film resurrected itself remarkably well. Listeners in Pakistan and the small-time cinema-goers in tier three and smaller towns were responsible for the remarkable recovery of the film. Now, *Aah* (1953) is reckoned as one of the all-time favourite classics of Nargis and Raj Kapoor.

Jaagte Raho (1956) was another small-budget movie with a message. It enhanced Raj Kapoor's status as a unique evolutionary filmmaker and actor. However, in the entire film, Nargis had no role to play, and this hurt the sentiments of the cine-goers. However, towards the end, she appeared in the film, and in many a small town, the film-goers erupted into applause and gave a standing ovation to 'Her Majesty of Indian Cinema'. Even though Nargis and Raj Kapoor never got married or indicated to get married, over the years, cinema-goers psychologically accepted them as a married couple. Their professional success partly dwelt on this perception.

The last film, before the unfortunate on and off-screen separation between Nargis and Raj Kapoor, was *Chori Chori* (1956). From the point of view of excellence in musical score, that year was a special year for music composers Shanker and Jaikishan. They composed the music for several masterpieces like *Yahudi* (1958), *Basant Bahar* (1956), *Halaku* (1956), *Raj Hath* (1956), *New Delhi* (1956), and *Patrani* (1956), but as far as the sales of records are concerned, *Chori Chori* (1956) beat them all, hands down. From the song *Aaja Sanam Madhur Chandni Mein* to others like *Panchhi Banoon Udti Phiroon, Yeh Raat Bheegi Bheegi, Man Bhavan Ke Ghar, Rasik Balma, Jahan Main Jaati Hoon,* all were great. This was a truly musical thriller. Somehow, the chemistry between Nargis and Raj Kapoor was at its best throughout the film. After seeing the movie, no one would have predicted that an all-of-a-sudden devastating breakup between the most successful actor and the most admired actor in the Hindustani film industry would have happened.

Professionally together since the days of the shooting of *Aag* (1948), when Nargis was less than 19 years old and Raj Kapoor was 23 years old, they had established a rarely-seen chemistry. Standing at five feet and seven inches in height, Raj Kapoor was on the shorter side for a Punjabi boy. Comparatively, as a five feet three and a half inches tall without shoes, Nargis was, by Indian standards, a reasonably tall woman. Yet, in all departments of film-making, they suited each other, and the films that they acted in together clicked exceedingly well at the box office.

Andaz (1949) gave Nargis the best chance to work closely with Dilip Kumar and Raj Kapoor and decide with whom to work more often in the future. Their breakup occurred after the completion and blockbuster release of *Chori Chori* more than seven years later, in 1956. For two highly sensitive artists who had a complete understanding of each other, it must have been a bolt from the blue, a heartbreaking experience. No one knew their state of mind. For millions of their fans, it was extremely shocking. Numerous big newspapers and tabloids throughout India carried stories about the unfortunate breakup. However, there were many who respected their privacy and did not indulge in idle gossip.

Both Nargis and Raj Kapoor enjoyed such an intimate and mutually respectful relationship that no one could, in their wildest dreams, have imagined their abrupt breakup. Many vendors in the film industry took their team for granted. Even Shanker and Jaikishan could not create music equal to their calibre for a few years after the breakup happened. They appeared once again in their real form in *Anari* (1959) and *Jis Desh Mein Ganga Behti Hai* (1960).

After the breakup, both tried to establish their credentials individually. Nargis produced her life's best acting performance in the film *Mother India* (1957). For this superlative performance, she won the Filmfare Award as the Best Actress in 1958. She was already 28 years old, and her marriageable age was passing very fast. She was more than willing to get married as quickly as possible. Despite very little time for marriage, she was lucky to get a very caring husband in young Sunil Dutt. This was even though her mother, a famous classical musician, married two Hindus in her life, and both had converted to the Islamic faith. Nargis exhibited her truly secular credentials by not insisting on Sunil Dutt's change of faith. Sunil Dutt appreciated the gesture. Even the names of his children were Hindu. Nargis made sure that their children followed the example of their parents and were also educated in elite English medium schools. Sanjay Dutt was educated in Sanawar, in a school near Kasauli in the then hills of Punjab (in 1966, it was merged with the hill state of Himachal Pradesh).

Sweetest Melodies, Sad Thoughts: Songs of the 50s

The fine art of filmmaking in India is not yet a century-old activity, as far as the talkies are concerned. The first talking film *Alam-Ara,* was released in 1931. Without knowing the requirements of the cinema-going public, the earliest film producers had a harrowing time zeroing in on the most appropriate lyrics, composers, and music directors to portray true romanticism. By the time India gained its independence, our film industry had attained its adulthood and matured enough to depict romanticism in song and dance sequences. By the beginning of the 1950s, a good number of Indian music directors had established a fine grip on the technique of creating sad and sweet romantic music of the finest order.

Some of our leading and professionally brilliant music directors of the pre and post-1947 era include Khem Chand Prakash, Anil Biswas, Sajjad Husain, Naushad Ali, Husan Lal Bhagat Ram, Sachin Dev Burman, Madan Mohan, C Ramchandra, Shyam Sunder and Shanker and Jaikshan. In this story, I am deliberately making no mention of Shanker

Jaikishan because they and their creations were mentioned in detail elsewhere in this book.

One epitome of a music maker's desire to depict romanticism was a song composed by Anil Biswas. In the film *Laadli* (1949), the lyrics were *Tumhare bulane ko ji chahta hai, Mukaddar banane ko jee chahta hai*. Behzad Lucknowi, a highly esteemed poet of romanticism, wrote them; the soulful tune was created by one of the best in the business, Anil Biswas, and it was rendered most romantically in the sweet, cultured voice of Lata Mangeshkar. This fine number, released in 1949, endures till today.

Another song rendered in the voice of Mukesh from the film *Aaram* (1950-51) is *Aye Jaan-e-jigar dil mein samane aja*. Its lyrics were composed by Rajinder Krishan, and the sad romantic tune was composed by Anil Biswas. It is indeed a landmark song. *Mil mil ke bichhud gaye nain, gaya sukh chain, judai chha gayi* are the opening lyrics of another song immersed in romanticism composed by Rajinder Krishan and musically fine-tuned by Anil Biswas for the same movie *Aaram*. Its unique appeal persists even today. The film *Tarana* (1951) was made with two heartthrobs, Madhubala and Dilip Kumar, in the leading roles. Its music composition was entrusted to Anil Biswas, who made sure that the film or its music attained new peaks of excellence. When the film was released, its most romantic music was applauded by the masses and the classes alike.

Khem Chand Prakash was a brilliant music director. Just one romantic song for the film *Mahal* (1949), *Aayega aane wala*, became the heart and soul of that movie. Its music ultimately amalgamated into the flawless personality of its highly admired female star. The song achieved what it aspired to achieve. Even today, people remember actress Madhubala and the romance in that song as the two ever-lasting memories of the film *Mahal*.

Sajjad Hussain was known for his romance with perfection in music. We can count the few Lata Mangeshkar numbers that she rendered for Sajjad Hussain on our fingertips. For the film *Khel* (1950), who can forget the romanticism in the song *Jaate hoto jao, hum bhi yahan, yaadon ke sahare jee lenge?* The film *Hulchul* was made in 1951, and Nargis was its soul. Who can forget the song *Aaj mere naseeb ne, mujhko rula rula diya, beete dinon ki yaad ne phir mera dil jala diya?* Sajjad Hussain was the soul of the song, and Nargis was the soul of romanticism. For the film *Saiyan* (1951), actress Madhubala was the soul of the movie, and Sajjad Hussain's music was the art of the movie. Similarly, no one can visualise the appeal of the film *Sangdil* (1952) without reference to the romanticism in the voices of Talat Mahmood and Lata Mangeshkar. Sublime was the romanticism in the melodies of Sajjad Hussain's musical compositions. One can say with certainty that the soul of the film *Rustom Sohrab* (1963) was the romanticism of two songs *Yeh kaisi ajab dastan ho gayi hai, chhupate chhupate bayan ho gayi hai* (Suraiya's voice) and *Aye dilruba, nazrein mila* (Lata Mangeshkar's voice).

Madan Mohan's class in music composition was much higher than that of his lesser rivals. His romanticism in musical tunes reflected the fragrance of the gardens of Iraq, Kurdistan, the Rawalpindi division of the northwest part of the Indian subcontinent, and the melting pot phenomenon of Bombay. If he created a true representation of love birds, it was in the song *Mera Qarar leja, Mujhe beqarar kar jaa, dum bhar to pyar kar jaa* (*Ashiana* 1951). Professionally, he was no less in *Dard ki aye raat guzar ja, aye dile-betab thehar jaa*. His symphony of love and longing unfolds meticulously in song *Aja kahin se aja, dil ka qarar leke, baithe hue hain kab se tera intzaar leke* (Film *Samunder* 1956). Who can forget the romanticism in *Tum ho saath raat bhi has seen hai, ab to maut bhi ka bhi darr nahin hai* (film *Mohar* 1959)? Madan Mohan's true hallmarks were the Urdu Ghazals he composed music for in films like *Adalat, Gateway of India, Railway Platform, Dastak* and *Jailor*.

Shyam Sunder brought his distinct flavour of romanticism in music from the Multan division of Pakistani Punjab into the drawing rooms of Bombay. *Baharein phir bhi aayengi, magar hum tum juda honge* (a melody picturised on Nargis in the 1949 film *Lahore*). *Saajan ki galiyan chhod chale, dil roya ansoo beh naa sake* (film *Bazaar* 1949) are just examples I am mentioning. Mohammad Rafi – Lata Mangeshkar duets par excellence was there too.

Among music directors, C. Ramchandra was considered a genius. Some of his most brilliant romantic tunes took just a few minutes to make. One of his most iconic tunes occurred to him while composing the music for the film *Patanga* in 1949. Its most captivating song is a Lata Mangeshkar number, *Thukra ke Mujhe o Jane wale, ik thokar aur lagata jaa, sindhoor to maang se cheen liya ab phoolon ko thukrata jaa, O jaane waale toone armaanon ki duniya lloot li, muskunane bhi naa payee thee tamanna loot li*. This song touches the inner chords of any romantically oriented listener. The film *Sagai* was also made in 1949, but its music was enjoyed in 1950. One of its Lata Mangeshkar numbers laments, *Dil ki kahani kehnaa to chahein, hai ri qismat keh na sake, ankhon se ansoo behna to chahen hai ri qismat beh naa sake*. A Madhubala–Dev Anand blockbuster film *Nirala* was made and released in 1949, and it continued well into 1950. One of its most popular Urdu Ghazal numbers was *Mehfil mein jal uthi shamma parvane ke liye, preet bani hai duniya mein mar jaane ke liye*, picturised on Madhubala and rendered by Lata Mangeshkar. It is still very popular all over the Hindi/Urdu-speaking Indian subcontinent.

The film Sipahiya was not very successful. One of its songs is romantically most appealing. It is *Hansi hansi naa rahi aur khushi khushi naa rahi*. All the songs rendered by Lata Mangeshkar for the film *Sangeeta* are superb and most romantic. Rendered by Lata Mangeshkar, these songs touch your heart. One particular song for the film *Hungama* is *Aye dard-e-mohabbat aa tujhko seene se laga kar pyar karoon*. Its tune, immersed in romanticism, is highly captivating. Though the film has gone into oblivion, yet this song survives for seven decades after its release. Some of the films for which C. Ramchandra composed the music have all the songs in the superhit class. These are films *Parchhayin, Saaqi, Yasmin, Azaad* and *Anarkali*. Not even one of their songs can be termed ordinary.

Pandit Husan Lal Bhagat Ram of village Kahma in Nawanshehar district of Indian Punjab constituted the first duo of professionally successful music directors who took the singers along remarkably well to create the most romantic effect with their musical compositions. Their first protégé was an actress/singer, Suraiya (also hailing from Punjab), for her immersed in sad renditions of the tunes they created by fully respecting her rich taste in music. She was not formally trained in classical music; therefore, she needed special attention, but the expression of subtle romanticism emerged naturally from her personality. During the 1948 to 1950 time frame, Suraiya churned out song after song in a highly emotional phase of life. Some of the Suraiya numbers had Mohammad Rafi as a male partner in duets. Some of the most versatile music rendered by Mohammad Rafi had the stamp of refinement he received from the personal coaching under the guidance of Pandit HusanLal.

Armed with a sweet, versatile voice, built over a sound foundation of classical music and powered by a very soft, sharp, shrill and flexible throat, Lata Mangeshkar came as an unseen phenomenon on the stage of Hindustani cinema in 1948. Pandit Husan Lal, who was at his professional peak then, took her as a protégé. Pandit ji discovered her to be a quick learner, ready to accept corrections as and when needed. Lata appeared at every training session well before the appointed time. Pandit ji would appear with his so-called weeping violin. Sitting in front of Lata ji, he would create the tune on the violin, and Lata Mangeshkar would respond with her vocal chords. Every tune would be finalised after a few rehearsals. Some of the most sad and romantic songs that came out of this Ustad–Shagird relationship: *Challe jana nahin nain mila ke saiyan bedardi; Chup chup khare ho zaroor koi baat hai pehli mulaqat hai ji pehli mulaqat hai; Jo dil mein khushi banker aaye, woh dard basakar chale gaye haaye chale gaye.* All these are from the blockbuster film *Badi Behan.*

Some other romantic songs of 1948 and afterwards are from the film *Adhi Raat* (1950) *Hamen duniya ko dil ke zhakham dikhlana nahin ata* (this is a Lata–Rafi duet). *Rona hi likha tha qismat mein hum geet khushi ke gaa naa sake* (a solo in the voice of Lata Mangeshkar). The film Meena Bazar was another great musical. I mention two special songs for the record. One is a highly romantic Mohammad Rafi–Lata Mangeshkar duet with the words *Paas aakar hue hum door, yehi tha qismat ko manzoor.* You can discern Husan Lal's sweet weeping violin in the interludes. The other song is a Lata Mangeshkar solo with the words *Ik din balam ik din zaalam, haaye dil bhi diya to kisko diya.* It is an immersed in sorrow song.

Film *Chhotti Bhabi* also had a great Mohammad Rafi–Lata Mangeshkar duet starting with the words *Khushi Ka Zamana gaya rone se ab kaam hai, pyar jiska naam tha judai uska naam hai.* The film *Aansoo* also had a very popular duet with the words

Sun mere saajna, dekho ji mujhko bhool naa jaana, sun mere sajna (voices of Mohammad Rafi and Lata Mangeshkar). It is still a very popular song.

One of the greatest Husan Lal Bhagat Ram musicals was the film *Afsana,* made in 1951. It has several outstanding songs, including some Lata Mangeshkar solos. One of them is *Aaj kuchh aisi chot lagi hai toot gaya paimana dil ka toot gaya paimana, koi nahin duniya mein apna, kaun sune afsana dil kaa, kaun sune afsaana.* Another highly melodious song is *Voh paas bhi rehkar pass nahin, hum door bhi rehkar door nahin.* Lata Mangeshkar sings it. One more song is *Abhi to main jawan hoon,* this is also a Lata Mangeshkar song, which has been used as a signature tune by Sri Lanka Broadcasting Corporation (popularly known as Radio Ceylon).

Romanticism was at its peak during the late 1940s and early 1950s in poetry and music of films; its standard has gone down lately and is experiencing a further decline in its quality. The golden era of melody and romance is indeed behind us. This book celebrates the golden era of film romance. For the younger generation, it offers an invitation to listen to the golden oldies with a computer tuned to YouTube with high-fidelity sound. If they mark the songs mentioned and listen to the golden oldies one by one, I am sure they will develop their taste for this music.

The Great Music Director, S. Mohinder

A sudden early morning call woke me up from my slumber. It was very sad news, which I was not prepared to receive. The oldest living music director of Bollywood and Pollywood, S. Mohinder (Mohinder Singh Sarna or Mohinder Singh Bakhshi), died on the morning of Sunday, 6 September 2020, due to old age-related complications, in Mumbai, at 4.45 a.m. His daughter, Nareen Kaur Chopra, who took care of him in his last years, informed me with a voice choked with emotions. He was also one of the few fully practising Sikh music directors in the film city of Mumbai during his lifetime. In a film industry full of scandals and sleazes, he was a non-controversial gentleman throughout his life. In a tribute to his memory, Lata Mangeshkar, in her Twitter message, described him as a perfect gentleman and a brilliant music composer. Lata Mangeshkar's younger sister, Asha Bhosle, who worked closely with him,

also had glowing words in his praise. Asha rendered a lot of songs and *shabads* under his music direction. At the age of 95, he was the last of the grand old guard of the golden age of film music in India. The most creative, sweetest, and most romantic film music of India was composed from 1932 onwards. He was the last one among the finest music composers that graced India in the 1940s and 1950s when there was a healthy rivalry among the best in the industry. He was an integral part of the galaxy of shining stars of that period. Nowadays, the absence of genuine melody in our film music, which the yesteryears abounded in, is definitely felt.

Since his childhood, S. Mohinder was exposed to the finest religious music in the gurdwaras of Lyallpur and Nankana Sahib. It was the Sikh devotional music that had a lasting impact on his taste for light music. He was one of the three music directors who learnt their skills from the gurdwaras. The first two were Master Ghulam Haider and Rashid Attre, both from Amritsar. Both were the sons of the musicians of the Golden Temple. S. Mohinder held Ghulam and Rashid Attre (Bhai Rashida) in very high esteem. He often talked about the captivating preludes and interludes in the songs composed by Master Ghulam Haider.

Almost 40 years ago, around 1982, seeing the virtual end of the best of his career, he started living mostly in the southern suburbs of Washington D.C. in the Virginia State of the USA. He lived there for 34 years until 2016. As time passed, he started missing his busiest days in Mumbai, where he had spent his youth and the most creative years of his life. For the last four years of his life (2016–20), he went back to Mumbai. From 1947 till date, most of the iconic music directors of Bollywood, including R. C. Boral, Timir Baran, Pankaj Mullick, Anil Biswas,

Khem Chand Prakash, Ghulam Haider, Rafiq Ghaznavi, Pandit Amar Nath, Husan Lal, Bhagat Ram, Vinod, Hemant Kumar, Hans Raj Behl, Naushad, S. D. Burman, Shanker-Jaikishan, Madan Mohan, Sardul Singh Kwatra, and Khayyam have died. S. Mohinder was the last of the all-time greats among music-makers to leave this world. With his death, an era came to an end. He was an icon worthy of being honoured even after death. It is saddening to point out that the Government of India did not bestow even the Padma Shri award on him.

S. Mohinder was born on 24 February 1925 in a non-descript village, Silanwala, in the then Montgomery district of the Pakistan portion of Punjab. Now, this district is called Sahiwal. He hailed from a family of ex-servicemen from the army background, though his father was a lawyer-police officer with a decent education. At the age of ten, his family moved to the neighbouring Lyallpur district of Pakistani Punjab, where his father was posted. This was the place where he learnt the basics of classical music, more precisely, religious music, from a very popular Sikh classical musician, Sant Sujan Singh, who later, after 1947, decided to settle in New Delhi (Karol Bagh and Rajauri Garden area) where he became immensely popular. S. Mohinder's family was originally from the Sargodha area of Rawalpindi division.

His father, Sujan Singh Bakhshi, was in the provincial police service of Punjab, serving as the prosecuting officer with the rank of inspector and above. A few years later, his family moved to Sheikhupura, the birth district of Sri Guru Nanak Dev ji, where he learnt the subtleties of classical music from the iconic Sikh religious musician Bhai Samund Singh ji *huzoori raagi*, Gurdwara Janam Asthan Sri Nankana Sahib. Since his father was in government service, the family kept moving from one station to the other. S. Mohinder's education started suffering due to his father's frequent transfers. So, he was enrolled, away from home, in Khalsa High School, Kairon, in the district of Amritsar. This school enjoyed a very good reputation then.

He was fiddling with the idea of becoming a radio artist, and in 1944, he was auditioned and approved as a radio singer at All India Radio Lahore, where, since 1945, he started performing once a month. There, in addition to Punjabi folk songs, he also rendered *shabads*. On one fateful day, he left Lyallpur in the morning to sing some songs at All India Radio. All seemed normal then. However, when he was returning from the radio station, he had to abruptly leave for India in a jiffy because of the serious communal rioting that erupted in Lahore, with fires raging in several Hindu-Sikh areas. Going to Lyallpur looked impossible, and he was compelled to board a waiting train for Mumbai, although he had a ticket to Lyallpur in his pocket and had no money to buy a ticket for Mumbai.

In Mumbai, he visualised his career as a music composer. Therefore, for a brief period, he underwent intensive training in classical music in the Mecca of classical music, the city of Varanasi, and subsequently returned to Mumbai to become a full-fledged

music director. For several years, he served as a salaried music director in the famous Filmistan Studios and Ranjit Studios. He composed music for some of the following films:

Sehra (1948), *Jeevan Saathi* (1949), *Nili* (1950), *Shrimati ji* (1952), *Veer Arjun* (1952), *Bahadur* (1953), *Paapi* (1953), *Naata* (1955), *Alladin Ka Beta* (1955), *Sau Ka Note* (1955), *Shahzada* (1955), *Sultan-E-Alam* (1956), *Shirin Farhad* (1956), *Karwan* (1956), *Patal Pari* (1957), *Sun To Le Hasina* (1958), *Khoobsurat Dhokha* (1959), *Do Dost* (1960), *Jai Bhawani* (1961), *Banke Sanwaria* (1962), *Reporter Raju* (1962), *Pardesi Dhola* (Punjabi) (1962), *Zarak Khan* (1963), *Captain Sheroo* (1963), *Sarfarosh* (1964), *Sunehre Kadam* (1966), *Professor X* (1966), *Picnic* (1966), *Nanak Naam Jahaz Hai* (Punjabi) (1969), *Man Jeete Jagjeet* (Punjabi) (1973), *Dukh Bhanjan Tera Naam* (Punjabi) (1974), *Teri Meri Ik Jindri* (Punjabi) (1975), and *Dahej* (1981).

He also composed music for some long-playing records of *shabads* made for special occasions and for some light Punjabi music albums as well.

He was fond of good eating, and just like another great music director, Madan Mohan Kohli, also hailing from the Rawalpindi division, he was a good cook, too. When guests arrived at his home, he took charge of cooking and had great pleasure in serving his hand-cooked dishes to his guests. When Dev Anand and Suraiya were in love, from 1949–51, they used to come to his office in the Filmistan Studios and talk to each other in solitude. They used to have intimate chats in chaste Punjabi, which the others did not understand. S. Mohinder did not want to disturb the love birds and pretended complete ignorance.

He was, particularly, an admirer of the brilliance of music directors Pankaj Mullick, R. C. Boral, Anil Biswas, Khemchand Prakash, Sajjad Hussain, C. Ramchandra, Husan

Lal, Bhagat Ram, Shanker-Jaikishan, Madan Mohan, and Jaidev. In his early years, Suraiya was his favourite female singer, and Mohammad Rafi was his preferred male singer. However, as time passed, Asha Bhosle became his favourite female singer. In hindsight, though, he felt that he made a big mistake in not patronising Lata Mangeshkar more. All his contemporary leading music directors like C. Ramchandra, Husan Lal-Bhagat Ram, Shanker-Jaikishan, Madan Mohan, Sachin Dev Burman, and Laxmikant-Pyarelal, who took Lata Mangeshkar as the primary singer for their sweetest compositions, gained immensely from her brilliance and popularity. Even music director Sardul Kwatra felt the same way. He also repented his minimal use of the most versatile voice of Lata Mangeshkar. O. P. Nayyar was the only music director who flourished without using her voice.

His music for a 1953 film, *Paapi*, became a nationwide hit. His most creative music, though, happened for the Madhubala-starrer historic romantic film *Shirin Farhad* (1956). It was critically appreciated by the fraternity of great music directors. Surprisingly, he had to wait until 1969 to receive the President of India's Award for composing the finest music for the year in the film *Nanak Naam Jahaz Hai*, which was released in 1969. This coveted award was bestowed on him in 1970. While in America, he composed non-film music for Asha Bhosle.

S. Mohinder had great regard for two female actors. The first one was actress-singer Suraiya, who was extremely respectful and obedient to her music directors. She respected S. Mohinder like her elder brother. The other was superstar actress Madhubala, considered the most beautiful actress of the Indian subcontinent. She did not believe in deceiving the people she was dealing with. Yet, every male she dealt with tried to take undue advantage of her. At one time, she was so frustrated with all the men around her that she had begun considering S. Mohinder as a perfect gentleman, maybe even the only one who was so.

Once, in fact, she even made an offer to marry him. This was despite knowing very well that S. Mohinder was already a happily married man. She made a highly lucrative offer regarding his wife's comfortable subsistence all her life and the finest schooling and college education for their four kids. S. Mohinder considered it very patiently but finally, after weighing the pros and cons, said no to her because he did not want to be unfair to his most faithful wife. (As narrated by S. Mohinder to me while in the USA.)

S. Mohinder told me another story about Madhubala. One day, during the 1960s, she was very sick and in pain. She called for him and requested him to take her to a gurdwara. S. Mohinder took her to one in Andheri. She bowed before the Holi Guru Granth Sahib and listened to *shabad* kirtan. At the end of the service, she cried and requested the head priest to suggest something to relieve her pain and agony. The priest told her that his religion does not suggest any rituals, but he advised her to do the *path* of *Japuji Sahib* and gave her a *gutka*. Madhubala did not know the Gurmukhi script. Hence, a special request was made to obtain an old Japuji Sahib Gutka printed in Persian script. The great actor started her daily *path* from it. She also sponsored *langar sewa* (service of free food) every year on the Parkash Gurpurab (birthday) of Guru Nanak Dev ji. As long as she was alive, she kept paying for the *langar sewa* on Guru Nanak's birth anniversary. Her father, Ata Ullah Khan, who outsurvived her by six years, continued the practice in the same gurdwara after

Madhubala died in 1969. Now, the management of the gurdwara pays for it. Even to this day, the free kitchen service on Gurpurab is performed in the name of Madhubala! Such was her charisma.

After 2016, S. Mohinder was back in India and was living with his daughter Nareen Chopra (Peoni) in Mumbai. He had difficulty talking and was very weak, but his memory was remarkably sharp. Peoni, who had known me since my days in New Jersey, kept me in the loop regarding his health and activities. In 2020, his health suddenly took a turn for the worse, and in the early hours of Sunday, 6 September 2020, he left this world.

He was a great admirer of the pioneer music directors of India and always loved to talk fondly about the likes of R. C. Boral, Pankaj Mullick, Timir Baran, Rafiq Ghaznavi, Jhande Khan, Khemchand Prakash, Ghulam Haider, Pandit Amar Nath, Pandit Gobind Ram, Anil Biswas, and Khawaja Khursheed Anwar. He had a photographic memory. He used to narrate some of the most interesting stories of his brilliant predecessors. In addition to Mohammad Rafi and Lata Mangeshkar, he was all praises for the voices of Noor Jehan, Manna Dey, and Talat Mahmood as well. Perhaps his greatest admiration lay for the versatile voice of Kundan Lal Saigal.

After the demise of another veteran music director, Khayyam, also a son of Punjab, he was the oldest living music director of the golden age of film music in India. He used to talk fondly about his music for films like *Shirin Farhaad* (1956), *Paapi* (1953), and *Nanak Naam Jahaz Hai* (1969). In *Shirin Farhad* (1956), his favourite song was a Lata Mangeshkar number, *Guzaraa Huaa Zamaana Aataa Nahin Dubaaraa Haafiz Khudaa Tumhaaraa.* For *Nanak Naam Jahaz Hai* (1969), it was two *shabads* that had been rendered in the voice of legendary Bhai Samund Singh ji, who was his mentor too. In addition, he particularly loved Guru

Gobind Singh ji's *shabad* sung by Mohammad Rafi, *Mittar Pyare Nu Haal Mureedan Da Kehna*. S. Mohinder's loss is a massive, lasting blow to the music industry of Bollywood. With his passing away, an era of great music direction has come to an end. He was indeed the last of the old guard of the golden age of film music in India.

All India Radio paid highly emotional tributes to him on its Vividh Bharati Channel. In addition, the Punjab-based programme originating and transmitting stations in Chandigarh, Jalandhar, Amritsar, Kasauli, and Fazilka presented their tributes to his everlasting memory as well. Sri Lanka Broadcasting Corporation, which has the largest library of film music in India, presented two special programmes in his memory. If he could not get a Padma Award while he was alive, he, for sure, deserves a Padma Award posthumously. This recommendation must be initiated by our political leaders in the Punjab Government, and the Centre should accord due respect to the state government's request.

Sajjad Hussain: The Perfectionist

Men of wisdom believe that genius is 90 per cent perspiration and 10 per cent inspiration. Very few people in this world are born great. Sajjad Hussain was one of those who attained greatness by virtue of his lifelong hard work, but his perpetually rebellious nature and short temper never let him attain his legitimately deserved spot in the history of his profession. Sajjad Hussain, by inspiration and perspiration, was a musician par excellence. He was born on 15th June 1917 in a Puritan musical family of a small urban agglomeration called Sitamau in Central India (now called Madhya Pradesh). Like several other musicians of his time, Sajjad Hussain's illustrious father, Mohammad Amir Khan, was perpetually a fiscally tight though professionally brilliant musician. True to his nature of being a hard taskmaster, Sajjad attempted to learn one of the most difficult ancient Indian instruments called the veena, which he mastered at a young age.

His first love was a Western instrument, the mandolin, which was totally unsuitable for playing the subtle intricacies of

North Indian classical music. To be able to play Indian ragas on the mandolin, one has to be a complete master at playing the instrument. Sajjad burnt the midnight oil to be able to play the Indian ragas to perfection on his mandolin. He attained working knowledge of playing several other instruments, both Indian and Western, before becoming a music director in the Hindustani film industry. He had a weakness for the piano, too, which was unavailable in villages and small towns at the time. When he left for Bombay, the piano was in great demand in film music, and he learnt it meticulously when he was in the city later. Sajjad mastered playing *tabla, dholak,* and *pakhawaj,* too.

There was no paucity of music directors; therefore, a cutthroat competition among the top music directors in India could be seen in both Bombay and Calcutta. R. C. Boral, Timir Baran, and Pankaj Mullick were mostly in demand as music directors in Calcutta. Bombay's leading music directors included Khem Chand Prakash, Anil Biswas, and Naushad Ali. In addition, there were new arrivals from Lahore (Shyam Sunder, Master Ghulam Haider, Pandit Husan Lal, Bhagat Ram, Pandit Gobind Ram, and Khursheed Anwar). Some of the others also came from Lahore after the Partition of Punjab.

As soon as Sajjad Hussain found himself capable and good enough to rub shoulders with those in the league of top-class music makers, he decided to put up permanently in the bustling city of Bombay—a melting pot where dreams and opportunities co-existed. To plunge into the thus far unchartered waters of composing music for the Bombay film industry, he first took baby steps towards becoming one of the hundreds of musical instrument players. For the first few years in the early 1940s, he had to be contented to be one of the little-known players of musical instruments in the orchestras of the already established film music directors. This was a stepping stone for graduating to the title of assistant music director and arranger of instruments. Very soon, his talent was noticed by the folks who mattered. His newly learned instrument, the piano, became his biggest asset. He used the piano extensively in his most successful film, *Sangdil* (1952).

His first independent assignment as a music director was for the film *Dost*, released in 1944. Although the superstar of the Indian film industry, Kundan Lal Saigal, was still alive, in this film, it was a little-known Kasur (Punjab)-born girl, Noor Jehan, an import from Lahore, who stole the limelight as a brilliant singer with her highly flexible God-gifted voice. Noor Jehan rendered three songs for this film, and all were difficult-to-render musical compositions with Sajjad Hussain's stamp of excellence. One of the songs with a very difficult tune was *Alam Par Alam Aur Sitam Par Sitam*, composed in a sad and slow beat. The entire credit for its success is owed to both Noor Jehan and Sajjad Hussain. The second song was *Koi Prem Ka Deke Sandesa*. This was a simpler and rather popular composition. The third song became a superhit; its opening words are '*Badnaam mohabbat kaun kare, aur ishq ko ruswa kaun kare*'. This was a special song that was on the lips of every cinema-goer and attained the top spot nationwide. Thus, Sajjad Hussian gained an outstanding opening, much better than his expectations.

Then came a series of films with great orchestration and lesser-known singers. The film *Dharm* was released in 1945, and Tilasmi Duniya hit the cinema screens in 1946. *Mere Bhagwan* was a moderate success in 1947. Then came *Qasam* in 1947, followed by a Suraiya and Surinder Nath-starrer film, 1857 (1946). This film unexpectedly broke new ground in 1946. Some of the Suraiya and Surinder Nath songs became very popular.

One of its most popular songs was a Suraiya-Surinder duet, *Teri Nazar Mein Main Rahoon*. Another solo by Suraiya was *Gham-e-Ashiyana Satayega Kab Tak*, and it became a very popular song.

Roop Lekha (1949) was also a moderate success. When Master Ghulam Haider discovered Lata Mangeshkar in 1947, he strongly suggested her playback voice to three top-of-the-line music directors—Khem Chand Prakash, Anil Biswas, and Sajjad Hussain. In due course, all of them gave a chance to his find, Lata Mangeshkar. Each one of them had a great success with this unusual shrill voice. Every popular female actor of the era gave a thumbs-up to Lata's voice.

One day, for a change, Sajjad Hussain was in a happy mood. This was around 1949. Sajjad happened to be talking to film playback singer Mohammad Rafi. He asked Mohammed Rafi, 'When you were in your childhood in your ancestral village in Amritsar, what kind of folk songs were you accustomed to singing?' Mohammed Rafi knew it all. He said that he used to sing either from Waris Shah's *Heer or* Peelu's *Mirza Sahiban*. Sajjad asked Mohammad Rafi to sing Heer, and he sang it smoothly. Sajjad Hussain told Mohammad Rafi that he was going to compose *Heer's* rendition in a different tune. After a few rehearsals, the new rendition of *Heer* was recorded, and it came out to be different and pleasant. A special 78 RPM disc was cut for this special rendition.

On the recommendation of another great music director, Anil Biswas, who had a great experience with Lata Mangeshkar in the films *Gajre* and *Anokha Pyar* in 1948, Sajjad Hussain gave Lata Mangeshkar a chance in the film Khel (1950). Some of the Lata Mangeshkar songs in the film came out to be outstanding. Earlier, Sajjad Hussain considered Noor Jehan as the best singer. But after trying Lata Mangeshkar's voice in Khel, his preference permanently tilted towards Lata Mangeshkar. One of Lata Mangeshkar's popular songs was *Jaate Ho To Jaao*. The other top song was *Bhool Ja Ae Dil Mohabbat Ka Fasana*. It was equally popular.

Meena Kapoor, the wife of music director Anil Biswas, used to rehearse very hard to render every song to perfection. One of the songs she rendered for the film *Khel* was *Tod Gaye Haye Tod Gaye*. This song turned out to be another hit song. Sajjad Hussain did an outstanding job in composing another tune for G. M. Durrani, in which the fading G. M. Durrani covered himself with glory in a very slow tempo. Its highly emotional wording is as follows: '*Apni mehfil mein phir ik baar chala aane de, teri mehfil ki baharon ko nahin chhedunga, tere toote huye taaron ko nahin chhedunga*'. This was perhaps one of the finest songs of G. M. Durrani. The music of the film Khel is one of the finest music ever composed by Sajjad Hussain.

After that, in his most popular films of the 1950s, it was Lata Mangeshkar who brought great name and fame to Sajjad Hussain. The film *Hulchul*, made in 1951, was another masterpiece of music maker Sajjad Hussain. Its song A*aj Mere Naseeb Ne Mujhko Rula Diya* became very popular. Another popular song was *Luta Dil Mera Haye Aabaad Ho Kar*. Sajjad Hussain could have composed more good music for this film had he not fallen out with its producer, who terminated the contract with Sajjad. The film *Hulchu*l had Nargis as its heroine and Dilip Kumar as the hero; both were top-of-the-line actors, and both were capable of ensuring a smooth path to success. But many times, there is a slip between the cup and the lip. This time, the slip was very costly.

In 1951, Sajjad Hussain composed outstanding music for the film *Saiyan*. Its top female star was Madhubala. She was accepted to be the prettiest film star of India by the entire industry. Most of the songs of Saiyan were considered masterpieces. Lata

Mangeshkar was the principal playback singer. The outstanding songs included *Kali Kali Raat Re Dil Bara Sataye; Hawa Mein Dil Dole, Machal Kar Bole; Voh Raat Din Voh Sham Ki Guzari Huyi Kahaniyan; Qismat Mein Khushi Ka Naam Nahin; and Khayalon Mein Tum Ho.* All these songs were graced with Lata Mangeshkar's sweet and shrill voice. The actor Madhubala liked all its songs. Even the producer liked the outstanding music. Sajjad was ecstatic at his own brilliant creation. He wanted some royalty from the profit of the film. The producer refused to share any profit with Sajjad. The quarrel went out of control, and the release of the film was delayed indefinitely. Eventually, after four decades, on the intervention of some well-wishers, including my good friend Chiranjiv Singh, IAS of Karnataka cadre, the film was released on videotape and other modes. The true lovers of music and the old-timers liked it. By the time of its release, the younger generation's taste of music had undergone a sea change. The younger generation was alien to this kind of music. A film which had the potential of getting a lot of film music contracts for Sajjad Hussain could not see the light of the day, and when it was released, the demand for such films was no longer there. This is nothing short of a tragedy.

Among the male voices, Talat Mahmood was Sajjad's most favoured voice. Even the Urdu poets liked his velvety, sweet voice. There was an imperceptible shiver in Talat Mahmood's voice, which was used to the hilt to portray deep romanticism by Sajjad Hussain and some other music directors. Sajjad's most successful film music assignment was the music of the film *Sangdil* (1952). In this film, two numbers rendered by Talat Mahmood are outstanding. One is sad and romantic with the opening words, '*Kahan ho kahan mere jeevan sahare, tujhe dil pukare*'; the piano plays a dominating role in it. The other one is highly romantic with the opening words, '*Ye hawa ye raat ye chandni, teri ek ada pe nissar hai*'. Some experts think that it is one of the best songs of the century. There is also an outstanding Lata Mangeshkar-Talat Mahmood duet in it. Its opening words include '*Dil mein sama gaye sajan, phool khile chaman chaman, pyar bhi muskura diya*'. One Lata Mangeshkar song was *Voh Toh Chale Gaye Aye Dil*. This was another all-time great number. Although the music assignment for the film *Sangdil* (1952) was not free of glitches, the contract nevertheless was completed and that too with distinction. Lata Mangeshkar gained from her performance in the film *Khel* (1950), and Talat Mahmood gained from his performance in the film *Sangdil*. His demand took a quantum jump, especially in Urdu films, which were very popular then.

In 1955, the film *Rukhsana* was made. Sajjad was never known for his love for the voice of Kishore Kumar, but for the film *Rukhsana*, he took Kishore Kumar as the male singer. Another surprise was his choice of Asha Bhosle as the preferred female playback voice. *Rukhsana's* music was a hit. One of its popular songs was *Tumhe Hum Yaad Karte Hain* in the voice of Asha Bhosle. Another popular duet was Yeh Chaar Din Bahaar Ke in the voices of Kishore Kumar and Asha Bhosale. Another masterpiece was *Tere Jahan Se Chal Diye Dete Huye Duaen Hum*, again, in the voices of Kishore Kumar and Lata Mangeshkar. Another beauty was T*era Dard Dil Mein Basa Liya*. An Asha Bhosale number was *Dil Ko Laga Ke Huzoor*. Another hit Asha Bhosale number was *Din Raat Jafayein Karte Hain*. The song *Tere Jahan Se Chal Diye Dete Huye Duaen* Hum was also recorded as a solo in Asha Bhosle's voice. In the meanwhile, several contracts were offered to Sajjad Hussain, but up to 1963, none reached fruition.

The last glimpse of Sajjad Hussain's magic was in the film *Rustam Sohrab,* made and released in 1963. Actor-singer superstar Suraiya once claimed that the last time she sang for Sajjad Hussain was in the film 1857 (1946), some good fifteen years ago. That film got its fame due to Suraiya's soulful renditions. Fifteen years later, too, its Suraiya number *Yeh Kaisi Ajab Dastan Ho Gayi* was film *Rustam Sohrab's* biggest hit. The other popular songs included a qawwali, *Phir Tumhari Yaad Aayi Ae Sanam* and a Lata Mangeshkar hit number *Ae Dilruba Nazrein Milaa.* One of the hit songs in the voice of Talat Mahmood, *Mazandaran Ajayi,* was noticed by the public; another hit song was *Ab Der Ho Gayi Vallah.*

After *Rustam Sohrab* (1963), although still at his professional best, Sajjad Hussain did not get any contracts for composing film music. His last professional assignment was the music for the film *Aakhri Sajda* in 1977. In his sunset years, he earned his livelihood by playing the mandolin in concerts in the big cities of India. With the passing years, his health was going down slowly, and on 21st July 1995, he breathed his last. His fans in the film industry came to his burial. It was a quiet, dignified affair. Radio Ceylon (Sri Lanka Broadcasting Corporation), Vividh Bharati

Mumbai, and the Urdu Service of All India Radio presented special tribute programs in his memory. Many regional capital radio stations also carried rich tributes to Sajjad.

Sajjad Hussain was very honest in his profession. He delivered what he promised. He never copied the work of other music directors. His music was pure and sweet, like mother's milk. All the playback singers were afraid of him. Even Lata Mangeshkar was scared of facing him. Talat Mahmood was often rebuked by Sajjad. He created a lot of music in anticipation of getting more contracts, which he never got. All that music is now lying with his sons. The authorities of Prasar Bharati should procure all this treasure and store it in the archives of Akashvani to be used by all the stations as and when needed.

Punjabi Cinema: From Lahore to Mohali via Mumbai

Punjabi cinema is only a few years younger than its Hindi counterpart, which dates back to the film *Alam Ara* (1931). The Punjabi movie industry made its successful debut in 1939, although some historians think it happened in 1935. Prints of the film *Gul-e-Bakavali* (1935), along with records of its music, are available. This film introduced Noor Jehan as a child actor. It was a cautious venture of a nascent Lahore film industry. The film was released in Lahore and Chitra cinema of Amritsar. Luckily, for a maiden venture, it did enough to stay afloat. Lahore was Punjab's cultural centre and the home for All India Radio Lahore, India's fifth—after the four metro area radio stations in Kolkata, Mumbai, Chennai, and New Delhi. This film clicked with the masses.

According to the Punjabi film industry's most comprehensive researcher, Mandeep Singh Sidhu, the first Punjabi film, *Ishq-E-Punjab (Mirza Sahiba)*, was produced in 1935. The other films produced, according to Mandeep Singh, included *Pind di Kudi*

(1936), *Heer Syal* (1938), and *Surdas* (1939). However, since I do not have any information on all of these films, their mention is omitted from this chapter.

According to Mandeep Singh Sidhu, the second, third, and fourth films of 1939 included *Mirza Sahiban, Pooran Bhagat, Sassi Punnu,* and *Sohni Mahiwal.* The films made in 1940, again, according to Mandeep Singh Sidhu, included *Ali Baba, Dulla Bhatti, Ik Musafir, Jagga Daku, Laila Majnu, Matwali Meera,* and *Mera Punjab.*

The next film worth mentioning is *Yamla Jatt* (1940), the plot of which was immersed in rural Punjabi culture. This film introduced Pran as the hero. It smashed previous records at the box office. Its mainstay was its music composed by Master Ghulam Haider Amritsari, which saw unprecedented success. Master Ghulam Haider discovered singer Noor Jehan in 1939 and Shamshad Begum in 1940. Later, in 1947, he stumbled upon the biggest discovery of life in Lata Mangeshkar in Mumbai.

In 1941, the films *Chambe di Kali, Chaudhary, Kurmai, Mera Mahi, Mubarak, Pardesi Dhola,* and *Sehti Murad* were made. In 1942, the films made were *Gawandi, Patola, Patwari, Ravi Paar,* and *Mangti.*

In 1942, *Mangti,* Punjab's first Lahore-produced superhit, became a silver jubilee film. It was released in all major cities of the undivided province like Ambala, Ludhiana, Jullundur, Ferozepore, Sialkot, Amritsar, Gujranwala, Lahore, Lyallpur, Multan, and Rawalpindi. Its music director, Pandit Gobind Ram, got nationwide publicity. Lahore's film industry discovered Pandit Amar Nath as a maverick music director in the 1940s. Later, Pandit Amar Nath trained his younger brothers, Pandit Husan Lal and Bhagat Ram, to become Bollywood's first highly successful duo of music directors during 1949–50.

In 1943, the Punjabi film, *Nakhattu,* was made. In 1944, *Koel* was produced, followed by *Gul Baloch* in 1945 and *Kamli* in 1946.

The sudden flare-up of the so-far simmering communal strife in the second half of 1947 dealt a crushing blow to the film industry of Lahore. All Hindus and Sikhs associated with the film industry had to make an unfortunate exit in August. The relocated Punjabi film industry tried to recreate another Lahore in the then city of Bombay.

The first post-1947 Punjabi film was shot in Mumbai and released in the country in 1948. It was titled *Chaman.* Those who saw it never missed the stamp of Lahori culture. The music was a masterpiece composed by Vinod, another import from Lahore. Two of its songs were re-recorded in the sensational voice of Lata Mangeshkar as an afterthought. Both weaved unique magic. Vinod later used Lata's voice to the hilt in the Punjabi film *Bhaiya Jee* (1950). Another music-maker, Hansraj Behl, exploited Lata's magic in *Lachhi* (1949). Allah Rakha did the same for *Madari* (1950) and *Phumman* (1951). The other Punjabi films that were made in 1950 included *Chhai* and *Mutiyar.* Films made in 1951 included *Balo* and *Baisakhi.* The two best films of 1953 included *Jugni* and *Kaude Shah.* In 1954, the films *Ashtali, Shah Ji,* and *Vanjara* were made. Both *Ashtali* and *Vanjara* had very good music. In 1958, *Nikki* also did well because of its good music. *Bhangra,* made in 1959, was a superhit too. After this, no Punjabi film did well for nearly ten years. All these years, Lahore's culture was alive through the Punjabi cinema of Mumbai.

Pakistan had good-looking actors. This helped to quickly re-establish the Lahore film industry. Also, what helped were music directors like Rashid Atre from Amritsar and G. A. Chishti from Jalandhar. Zubaida Khanum, a budding female singer of Amritsar, became Pakistan's substitute for Lata Mangeshkar and Shamshad Begum. Soon, Noor Jehan joined from Mumbai, and the film centre of Lahore started buzzing with activity. Between 1950 and 1960, Lahore's Punjabi film industry had a very successful run.

For a few years, the Punjabi film industry in Mumbai maintained its strict Lahori culture and was a success. However, as time passed, the melting pot of Mumbai had its impact. The hybrid culture-induced degradation started after *Jugni* (1953), *Vanjara* (1954), and *Bhangra* (1959). Up to 1979, hybrid Punjabi-Mumbai culture could not keep its appeal with the indigenous home-spun Punjabis back home, and the films lost their profitability. *Nanak Naam Jahaz Hai* (1969) was an exception due to its pure appeal to religious sentiments. It was also produced by Amritsaris—the Maheshwari brothers.

Then, a big experiment at Punjabi Art Cinema was attempted in the form of *Chann Pardesi* (1980) and *Long Da Lishkara* (1983). Both met the expectations of cinema-going Punjabis. Mohammad Rafi sang his last Punjabi song before his death for the film *Chann Pardesi* (1980). Thus, a brand-new local film industry started taking shape in the Chandigarh-Mohali belt. Comedian Jaspal Bhatti also introduced a composite Amritsari-Chandigarh-based comedy entertainment show, *Ulta Pulta*. His sudden death in an accident a few years ago snatched away a new form of urban touch from the East Punjabi film business.

Of late, the Punjabi cinema industries of Lahore and Mohali seem to be drifting apart. The language is getting different. Lahore is still dominated by Central Punjabi, the language of the Lahore-Amritsar belt. But Mohali cinema, barring a few exceptions like *Angrej* (2015) and *Lahoriye* (2017), now mostly represents the rural Malwa culture, which has evolved from the non-refugee new settlers in the greater Chandigarh area. This no-frills, real-life-based cinema is finding widespread acceptance in India. However, it may not be necessarily so in Pakistan. On the music front, I have observed that Pakistani Punjabi cinema has better music directors and better voices. On the contrary, due to the low-cost character of Indian Punjabi films, our singers are inexpensive, and the music, too, is cost-cutting. The number of instruments used in Indian Punjabi cinema is also comparatively lesser. In the Indian Punjabi film *Lahoriye* (2017), a short clip of Pakistani singer Shaukat Ali was introduced, which markedly enhanced the appeal of the film.

One good news is that the highly lucrative markets for the films shot in the Mohali area are opening in Canada, the USA, the UK, Italy, Australia, New Zealand, and the Middle East. The second positive signal is the advent of new actors like Gippy Grewal, Binnu Dhillon, Karamjit Anmol, Jaswinder Bhalla, Diljeet Dosanjh, Amrinder Gill, Tarsem Jassar, Ammy Virk, Mehtab Virk, Satinder Sartaj, Amberdeep, Neeru Bajwa, Sargun Mehta, Anita Devgan, and Satinder Satti, to name a

few. Veterans like Nirmal Rishi, Yograj Singh, Guggu Gill, B. N. Sharma, Rana Ranbir, and Gurpreet Ghuggi are getting newer recognition. Some Punjabi films that have been shot in Mohali recently include *Angrez* (2015), *Lahoriye* (2017), *Manje Bistre* (2017), *Golak Bugni Bank Te Batua* (2018), *Ardas* (2016), *Sajjan Singh Rangroot* (2018), *Subedar Joginder Singh* (2018), and *Daana Paani (2018)*. Punjab has turned the corner in making period films. These films do not cost much to produce but are all returning huge dividends. This newly emerging industry will, eventually, give a big boost to the economy of the region around Chandigarh. Technical processing of these Mohali films is still being done in Mumbai. However, once it establishes its units in the state capital region, there will be a boom in business. For now, a not-shot-in-Mohali but highly successful film is *The Black Prince* (2017), the story of the last king of Punjab, Maharaja Duleep Singh.

In cinema's sister profession, theatre, Lahore has been the capital for over one hundred years. Amritsar was close behind. After the partition of 1947, Amritsar has forged ahead in East Punjab. With five highly active theatre groups performing regularly in the city, Amritsar has undoubtedly become the 'Theatre Capital of East Punjab'.

The way experimentation in Punjabi cinema is going on in Mohali, we can look towards a very bright future for Punjabi cinema.[1]

1. Previously published in *The Tribune*.

Part-II

RADIO

Enchanted By the Sound of Music

I am taking you 89 years back. After finishing his studies in London, my father sailed back to India by the end of 1931. After a few days on the high seas and after squeezing through the Suez Canal, his ship docked in the Mumbai harbour, and he took a train to reach Punjab.

Despite World War I, imperial England was a flourishing and advanced country. The Londoners were accustomed to a host of modern facilities like trains, theatre, cinema, and radio. Domestic radio broadcasting was firmly established in London to provide the latest news and entertainment.

On return to our village, Aujla, my father decided to buy a gramophone to satisfy his immense love for music. Radio had already arrived by then. He searched the entire Sadar Bazaar in Kapurthala and could not find a shop selling records and gramophones.

A few months later, he took a trip to Amritsar to buy a gramophone. The biggest stockist of gramophones and records in Hall Bazaar, surprisingly, did not have a single compact briefcase-type gramophone in stock. All that the store had was a couple of bulky gramophones with huge brass speakers. That was not the requirement of my father.

The author with his parents

The shop owner said he was expecting a big consignment of gramophones and records from His Master's Voice company in Kolkata, but my father had made up his mind and was in a hurry to purchase one. He left the shop in a jiffy and took the next train to Lahore.

Anarkali Bazaar was the biggest and the most fashionable shopping area in Lahore. My father saw several compact gramophones in black and brown khaki exteriors in its music shop. Since the villages were dusty, he picked up the one in brown colour. One of the salesmen demonstrated its simple operation.

My father liked it and got it under ₹100. He received a couple of complimentary records as well. K. L. Saigal was a reigning superstar then. The records were in his voice.

On reaching home, my father opened it to play it for my grandmother. As soon as the sound of the music was heard, a crowd gathered. Those who listened were wonder-struck to hear something so unheard of.

The news of a talking machine reached the neighbouring villages, too. There were some Muslim professional musicians, called *rababis*, in our village. Many a time, they would bring old records of great musicians from their acquaintances in Kapurthala, Sultanpur Lodhi, and Jalandhar to listen. After a year, the wealthiest man in the village, Baba Inder Singh, an uncle of my father and a minister in the government of Maharaja Jagatjit Singh of Kapurthala, bought another gramophone. Perhaps it was from France. To our relief, this new addition diverted a lot of the attention away from our gramophone.

After another five years, in 1937, along with Kolkata, Mumbai, New Delhi, and Chennai, another station of the AIR came up in Lahore. This new radio station became a craze.

Our old gramophone, now aged 90, is still with me. It looks worn out but works, nevertheless. On my part, I have decided to retire it gracefully. In its youth, when we were kids, it played thousands of records and pleased many a heart. Now, in perfect solitude, it rests, maybe reminiscing on its golden days. Once in many months, I still play it for the sake of nostalgia. Some memories are forever.[1]

---

1. Previously published in *The Tribune*.

Radios: From Bulky Drawing Room Showpieces to Miniaturised Pocket-Sized Gadgets

After the invention of Edison's phonographs – playing barrel-shaped records hung on horizontal rods, Berliner's gramophones in the 1880s, and later playing 78 RPM (Revolutions Per Minute) ten-inch diameter flat records – the next biggest invention in sound reproduction was that of the radio transmitters and receivers, which pulled the radio waves from transmitters located miles away and reproduced lifelike sound for the pleasure and knowledge of the listener. Europe led the research initially, and England was at the forefront of the nations that manufactured radios.

America, due to its well-known prosperity, always thought and did big things. The earliest radio receiver sets made in America, hence, were built from hard, heavy, and expensive timber. They were meant for resting on the floor in the rich man's massive living (drawing) rooms. Mass manufacture of radios in the USA started in the second half of the 1920s, and production kept increasing exponentially year after year. The earliest radios were built into exotic shapes, and some were minutely carved by hand from hard and expensive timber. The lighted tuning dials were made into lovely shapes and sizes. The oldest radios were built into wooden cabinets made primarily out of rose and cherry wood.

When Marconi invented the radio, he used a limited wave band spectrum for his broadcasting necessities. He and his competitors used wavelengths roughly between 200–500 m. In terms of frequency, they worked between 1,500–1,600 kilocycles/second. Later, the term kilocycles/second was given a new name—kilohertz (kHz). As research advanced, this oldest spectrum was addressed as a medium-wave. Some called it amplitude modulation. America uses a huge range of medium-waves starting from 530 kHz to 1,680 kHz or even 1,700 kHz for its domestic use with a frequency differential of 10 kHz between two adjacent frequencies. The rest of the world uses a slightly smaller spectrum with a 9 kHz frequency differential. Canada and Mexico, being America's neighbours, are also more or less using the American spectrum. The rest of the world must be contented with a restricted medium-wave spectrum with a slightly narrower bandwidth and marginally poor sound quality.

Europe, and to some extent America, too, is using another spectrum called long-wave, whose range falls between 30–300 kHz. This is also called the low-frequency spectrum. The long-wave propagates through ground waves, which bend with the hills and dunes. Its signal can reach 1,200 miles or 1,900 km at night and can be picked up from sunken ships in salt water. However, for most of the world, long-wave is still alien. However, old radios in several countries had long-wave.

The Frequency Modulation (FM) band using 88–108 MHz spectrum is getting immensely popular all over the world these days because of its broader bandwidth and point-to-point communication technique. Its sound is clearer, crispier, and more realistic and during periods of bad weather, its reception remains unfazed. It evolved as a by-product of the worldwide research for television. FM has already dealt a fatal blow to the short-wave and has started hurting the medium-wave as well. Early radio receivers, capable of catching the medium-wave, long-wave, and short-wave signals from far away European nations, with the help of aerials, were floor pieces.

The picture shows a made-in-Germany 1957 five-band Telefunken radio, including three short-waves, one medium-wave, and one FM band. During its heydays, it was one of the most elegant radios in the world. During those days, there was tough competition between Grundig and Telefunken.

A 1957 five-band Telefunken radio

During the 1990s, after the substantial cooling down of the Cold War between the United States and the erstwhile Soviet Union, the use of expensive short-waves diminished all over the world. Due to the waning popularity of short-waves, the size and the beauty of the radio receivers are also taking a big hit. Barring its use in cars, radio today has become less popular except in the remote areas of the African continent.

The old-fashioned valve radios used to be bulky. This species started vanishing in Europe and North America during the mid-1950s. In India, however, they continued to manufacture them until the mid-1960s. The beauty of the wooden cabinet also came to an end with the phasing out of tube or valve radios. These old vintage beauties are now gracing museums all over the world.

In the USA, the golden period of large and beautiful-looking radios started in the 1930s, when radio receivers were mass-produced, and there were record sales of these sets. At the same time, radio stations were multiplying all over the USA, and radio transmitters were also being manufactured in large numbers, not only in the USA but in the continent of Europe as well. Some of the earliest and most elegant-looking radios, though, were manufactured in the USA.

Floor-mounted American Radio Philco

This period lasted through the Second World War and started fading with the advent of television sets. The radios produced in this period were the most beautiful and expensive. The golden age of radios in Europe followed in America. Here, too, it lasted from the 1930s to the end of the Second World War. Television proliferated in Europe after the Second World War, but due to the destruction of European prosperity in the war, the growth of television was slower in Europe, and that indirectly gave chance for radio to proliferate on short-wave. The Europeans, after 1945, built the most magnificent short-wave radios with an increasing number of short-wave bands. The more the short-wave bands, the larger the size of the radio. The large size, in turn, enhanced the beauty of the receiver sets. Although the economy of Europe took a big hit during the Second World War, the demand for radios kept increasing

Vintage Philco Lowboy Console Radio, Model 87, AM Band, 8 Vacuum Tubes, Made In USA, Circa 1929–1930

even during the dreadful war. Due to its location being away from Europe, America was, more or less, unaffected by the Second World War.

The radio in the picture was one of the most elegant American radios made in the 1930s and 1940s. These radios did not have FM but included short-wave and medium-wave bands.

Today, some vintage floor-mounted radios are considered a piece of art. Most of these radios belonged to the rich in America. The Europeans had smaller, and more compact houses, and that was reflected in the size of their radios, too. The nations of the Soviet Union were obsessed with short-wave because, in length and breadth, it was the largest country in the world. They, thus, manufactured their radio receivers with a minimum of two short-wave bands. These two short-waves consisted of 13, 16, 19, 25, and 31 m in one band and 41, 49, 60, 75, 90, and 120 m in the second. In addition, they had one medium-wave. This was the base model. The most common Soviet Union radios included four bands—the first short-wave included 13, 16, 19, and 25 m, the second included 31, 41, 49, and 60 m, and the third carried all the tropical bands from 60 to 120 m bands, plus one medium-wave band. The largest and most stylish radios had separate short-wave bands for 13, 16, 19, 25, 31, 41, 49, 60,

Stewart Warner O1-6D4 Table Radio

75, 90, and 120 m, plus one medium-wave band. Later, 11 m and 22 m were also added. During the 1950s, FM was also added to the new radios made in the Soviet Union. From the point of view of sound, the Russian-made radios were a poor cousin of the German and Dutch (Philips) radios. In terms of the quality of sound, even the British radios were far better.

Some of the radios had record players or record changers added to them and were bulkier. They played all sizes of records. The smallest records were seven inches (45 RPM), the medium-size records included ten inches (78 RPM), and the largest were the 12 inches (one-foot diameter) 33.33 RPM long-playing records. The largest ones could play between 35–40 minutes. The duration of the seven-inch records was between six to seven minutes, and some were even of three minutes duration. The ten-inch records with 33.33 RPM speed could play for 25–30 minutes. Gerrard Company of Germany was the biggest manufacturer of radiograms, record players, and record changers.

A floor-mounted composite American radio with a phonograph

Shown in the picture is a floor-mounted composite American radio that also had a phonograph built into it to play records. Radio came to India very late. Earlier attempts to establish private radio stations by radio clubs in the metropolises of Kolkata, Mumbai, Madras (now Chennai), and Lahore during the 1920s and early 1930s failed miserably. However, when All India Radio started in 1936–37 with the participation and control of the government in the cities of Kolkata, Mumbai, New Delhi, Chennai, Lahore, and Peshawar, the number of radio sales took a quantum jump. This was the period when beautiful-looking radio receivers of Philips and Murphy were assembled in India.

Then came the most horrifying rioting and the destruction of the province of Punjab and the Bengal Presidency in 1947. The golden days of radio started in India in the 1950s, when radio stations were set up in every province (later state), and radio receivers were mass-produced. This age continued until the rapid expansion of short-wave and abruptly ended with the Government of India's sudden decision to rapidly spread television throughout the length and breadth of sub-continental India. FM radio expanded by piggybacking on its more popular cousin, Doordarshan, in and after the 1990s in all parts of India. The masts for antennae built for Doordarshan transmitters

Manufactured in Holland and assembled in India, Phillips Radio.

fulfilled the dual purpose of serving the FM transmitters antennae, too. It can be said that FM in India took advantage of the infrastructure that was created for television.

The radio in the picture was one of the most beautiful and powerful radios assembled in India. It had four short-wave bands, including a full tropical band plus medium-wave, displaying nine-kilohertz frequency differentials. There was no long-wave and no FM band because India was not using either of the two.

A kid listening to a floor-mounted radio in America

Radio stations mushroomed all over America throughout the 1920s. The European countries were a little sluggish in expanding their radio broadcasting services. Their manufacturing took off after 1925. To receive broadcasts with realistic quality sound, wealthy Americans started buying bulky radio sets with huge speakers. They used the most expensive and durable wood. The radios were priced based on the quality of wood used and the size and quality of speakers used. Generally, huge-sized woofers were used in this kind of radio to produce the sound of church-quality instruments.

GEC BC4655, 1946

The first big-scale import of radio receivers into India was of the radios manufactured by the General Electric Company (GEC) of England. These were midsized tabletop radios. The radio receiver shown in the picture is a rare piece with a unique shape. It can work on AC and DC electric supply. Its sound, given its size, was absolutely mesmerising. These radios proved very popular. In the late 1930s, the British radios started being assembled in India. Philips Company of Holland (Netherlands) started assembling radios in India during the 1940s.

A made-in-Germany Grundig 960 radio

As mentioned above, the first radio receivers in America were heavy wooden sets placed on the floors. Some of the radios were as tall as three to four feet above the floor, and in width, they were a little more than two feet. The valves that caught the waves were also bulky. Some were the size of an electric bulb! The consumers wanted deep, concert-hall-style sounds, like in an orchestra. For this, what was needed was the best high-wattage amplifiers and large-size speakers. In some cases, the size of the woofer was 12 inches in diameter and sometimes even more. Some tweeters were installed to produce clarity of sound as well as to produce higher and shriller notes. The size of the speaker determined the width of the radio set. Generally, very expensive wood that had a long life, like mahogany, teak, cherry, rose, and walnut, was used for making cabinets for these radio sets. The finished wooden cabinets were carefully polished to give a shining brownish look.

The floor-mounted radios took up a lot of showroom space. This was a big drawback. The next generation of radios manufactured in America during the 1940s were, hence, tabletop radios. The width of these radios was not reduced, but the height was reduced to less than half compared to the earlier ones. With time, the valve radios also became slimmer.

During the mid-1950s, small, transistorised radios started coming into the market. This started the trend of miniaturisation of radios. The first valve-less radios were about 12 inches wide and about eight to nine inches high. The depth ranged from three to four inches. As time passed, the size started getting smaller. Today, short-wave is being eliminated, and only AM/FM radios are becoming more popular. The miniaturisation of radios is happening so fast that, now, some radios can even fit into pockets! The base notes are becoming the casualty, but the sound is clearer and crispier.

A Grundig Satellit 700 radio manufactured in Germany

In the early 2000s, in the USA, I personally saw some old radios manufactured in the 1930s. Neither their finish had deteriorated nor had their overall look changed. Some of the most popular American radios were selling under the brand names GE (General Electric), Emerson, Admiral, Crosley, Zenith, Magnavox, and Majestic.

The tuning dials of different brands were in several sizes and configurations. Some were barely four inches wide, while others were bigger and wider. Some of the dials were in the form of a needle moving in a semi-circular movement around a pivot.

Panasonic RF2900 radio manufactured in Japan

Sony ICF2010 radio manufactured in Japan

One of the most powerful and sensitive world-band radios is the Sony ICF 2010 tabletop radio. It can lock frequencies and can receive the USB (Upper Side Band) and LSB (Lower Side Band) broadcasts, which are power-saver and bandwidth-saver alternatives in high-powered SWs.

One of the latest digital Sony radios manufactured in Japan

I saw a green-coloured magic eye in most of the large short-wave radios. The radio receivers manufactured in Europe were smaller compared to those made in America. Some were more in width than in height. Some of the radios manufactured in Europe were made of bakelite material. Most of these were not floor-mounted. The size of the radio speakers of European countries was much less than 12 inches in diameter. GEC radios were manufactured in the United Kingdom, as were the Pie, Dixon, and Frente radios. The Netherlands manufactured radios under the brand name Philips. The Germans manufactured their radios under several big names, such as Grundig, Telefunken, Gerrards, and Seamons, among many others. The radios manufactured in Germany now include Blaupunkt, too, which has the finest high-note sound.

The miniaturisation of radio receivers has several advantages. The first is its small size and lesser weight. Another advantage is that its speakers are really small, and their sound is great for their size. Also, the transistors or the printed circuit last much longer than the circuitry of the old valve radios.

Sangean SG-110 AM/FM Stereo Pocket Radio

The new car radios have large, high-powered speakers. They can accommodate CDs and USBs and can work with Bluetooth. Since TVs are a distraction for the drivers and passengers in cars, no country can allow the installation of TVs in cars. Therefore, car radios are getting more sophisticated and expensive. These days, several radio stations in European and American cities are giving weather reports and conditions of traffic. Routes can be planned by taking traffic conditions into account. Some manufacturers of car radios are omitting even the medium-wave from their radios. This is being done to avoid weather-related disturbances.

Ciglow Digital FM Radio, Mini AM/FM 2 Band Stereo Pocket Radio Receiver with LCD Display and Earphone

For the convenience of radio listeners, I am sharing my expertise attained through years of listening in the flatlands of Punjab and the hill areas in northern India and the USA. The following table is based on the strength of transmitters commonly used in the world:

MEDIUM-WAVE

The night time medium-wave transmitter range can easily increase by five to ten times depending on the clarity of the weather and the hour of the night.

Power in kilowatts (kW)	Range in miles during day time
1	15
5	20
10	25
20	35
50	60
100	80
200	125
300	155
500	200
1,000	350

Power in kilowatts (kW)	Range in miles during night time
1	100
5	200
10	350
50	600
100	1,000
200	1,500
300	1,800
500	2,200

FM ranges

In the case of FM transmitters, the power of the transmitter is more or less inconsequential. The only advantage of more power is that it prevents blocking by rival stations. It becomes more difficult to block transmissions if the power of the transmitter

Height of the tower above the ground	Range in miles
100 feet	14
200 feet	20
328 feet (100 metres) 10 kW transmitter	35
656 feet (200 metres) 10 kW transmitter	50
984 feet (300 metres) 10 kW transmitter	62
1312 feet (400 metres) 10 kW transmitter	65
1649 feet (500 metres) 10 kW transmitter	70

Height of the tower above the ground	Range in miles
2500 feet 10 kW transmitter	80
5000 feet 10 kW transmitter	95
6500 feet 10 kW transmitter	102
8000 feet 10 kW transmitter	110

1931 Philco Model 90 Cathedral Radio

is much higher than the one trying to block it. In the plains, for larger cities, as well as in the twin cities, it is recommended to use tall towers. Some countries are using 30 kW and higher strength transmitters, too. The best transmitters for optimum utility are the 10 kW power transmitters.

President Franklin D. Roosevelt used to listen to a cathedral-style (as shown in the picture) radio during the Second World War. Short-wave transmissions are the most difficult for making predictions of range. Scientists are working day and night to determine the range of short-wave transmitters, but so far, they are out of luck. On some days, a low-powered short-wave transmitter can cross halfway around the world to be heard satisfactorily. In many cases, the most powerful transmitters cannot reach their normal expected range. Given below is a table of the power of the transmitters and their anticipated range based on my lifelong research:

Tecsun PL-660 Digital Shortwave Radio

Power of the short-wave transmitters in kW	Range in miles
10	500
50	1,000
100	1,600
200	2,100
500	3,000

The power of short-wave transmitters with kilowattage beyond 500 kW is disallowed all over the world because of this situation a lot of countries have curtailed or discountinued their short-wave services. Since most of the nations have already shut down their short-wave transmitters. This has removed congestion on the short-wave bands. because of which the clarity of short-wave transmissions has improved, and the range has increased. In future, my research on this subject shall continue.

Radio towers on Sandia Peak

Frequencies of some important FM Radio Stations in India

New Delhi	100.1 FM 102.6 FM Rainbow 106.4
Chandigarh	107.2 (Via Kasauli high altitude)
Jalandhar	102.7 100.6 Vividh Bharti 100.8 Fazilka 100.9 Kasauli (high altitude) 103.6 Amritsar (High powered low altitude) 100.1 Ferozepur (low powered) 100.1 Gurdaspur (low powered)
Amritsar	103.6 (High powered low antenna)
Ludhiana	100.1 (High powered)
Patiala	100.2
Bhatinda	101.1
Shimla	103.7
Dharamshala	103.4
Kullu	102.5
Hamirpur	101.8
Lucknow	101.6
Kanpur	107.1
Kanpur	103.7
Aligarh	101.3
Amethi	103.1
Faziabad	101.9
Hardoi	100.1
Jhansi	103
Lakhmipur Kheri	102.3

Mathura	102.2
Meerut	101.7
Rai Barreli	102.8
Rampur	102.9
Hissar	102.5
Rohtak	103.5
Kurukshetra	101.4
Alwar	103.1
Banswara	101.3
Chitaurgarh	102.9
Churu	100.7
Jaipur	100.3
Jaiselmer	101.8
Jhalawar	103.2
Jodhpur	102.1
Mumbai	100.1
Mumbai	102.8
Pune	101.0
Nagpur	100.6
Aurangabad	101.7
Bhopal	103.5
Pachmarhi	100.1
Jabalpur	102.9
Ujjain	102.5
Gwalior	101.8
Indore	101.6
Patna	101.6
Muzaffarpur	100.4

Talking to the People of Pakistan

The largest chunk—60 per cent—of the population of Pakistan lives in the province of Punjab, out of which most speak Punjabi. We can confidently say that at least 50 per cent of Pakistanis understand and converse well in the Punjabi language. All other linguistic groups are much smaller. Roughly ten per cent of Pakistanis speak Pashto, another ten per cent speak Balochi, and 20 per cent speak Sindhi. Urdu is the mother language of only 10 per cent of Pakistanis, but 40 per cent of educated Pakistanis do know this language and can converse in it. About 20 per cent of well-educated people in Pakistan understand English, too, and they are the most influential in the country.

India's most difficult neighbours are Pakistan and China. China can be covered on short-wave only. India broadcasts to Pakistan in Urdu, Sindhi, Pashto, Punjabi, Saraiki, and Balochi languages. Whereas the other languages get their due, Punjabi, the most used language, does not get the respect it deserves. My assessment is that the Punjabi language has been given a raw deal. At present, there are only two hours of programming of All India Radio in Punjabi, and that, too, does not reach the entire West Punjab. Until recently, it was carried by a poor-quality medium-wave transmitter and an FM transmitter that did not work at its full strength due to a very short transmitting antenna. All other services were carried out, until recently, on short-wave. However, only Punjabi never received a short-wave transmitter. Until India finds a substitute for short-wave, it must use its vast network of presently idle short-wave transmitters. For Punjabi service, the transmitters located in the Delhi-Aligarh belt can provide one-hop, excellent signal strength in West Punjab in its entirety.

Three different transmissions in the Punjabi language are proposed. The morning service should be from 6 a.m. to 8 a.m. It should be carried on 49, 41, and 31 m bands. The noon service should be from 12.30 p.m. to 2.30 p.m., and it should be carried on 16, 19, and 25 m bands. The nightly service should be from 9.30 p.m. to 11.30 p.m. It should be transmitted on 49, 41, and 31 m. As the propagation conditions change, these frequencies can change with them. These wave bands are being suggested for sunspot numbers ranging from as low as 20 to as high as 200. The FM transmitters of Amritsar should carry all the transmissions as FM is unaffected by sunspot numbers.

The presently serving FM transmitter carries mostly Urdu service. We need a new FM transmitter for the expanded Punjabi service, preferably of the same power as the existing transmitter. For the rest of the duration, it can carry the programming of Vividh Bharati, FM Gold, or the primary channel of All India Radio Jalandhar. To obtain the best results, the programmes of the Punjabi service should originate in New Delhi. Simple words of the Urdu language can be incorporated into the Punjabi translation, and the most difficult Farsi or Arabic language words should be translated into Punjabi. The broadcasters should be recruited from Amritsar, Batala, Tarn Taran, or Gurdaspur. Two or three of them should be posted in Amritsar to monitor the broadcasts coming from Pakistan and to dispatch them to New Delhi. Another group of six broadcasters should be stationed in New Delhi close to the office of the Urdu service. The music to be broadcast should be equal to 50 per cent of Pakistani and 50 per cent of Indian artists. The language should be Central Punjabi, popularly known as standard Punjabi, spoken in the old undivided districts of Gujarat, Gujranwala, Sheikhupura, Sialkot, Lahore, Amritsar, Ferozepur, and Gurdaspur. The programmes should be linked from New Delhi and downlinked at the transmitter site at Gharinda (Amritsar).

To obtain the best results during eventualities, a new, strongly-built, bomb-resistant, and reinforced cement concrete tower of at least 500 m in height should be built. It should have a high-altitude office towards the top of the tower. In the meanwhile, the existing 300 m high steel tower should be used after its partial reconstruction to correct deformities. It will increase the range of coverage at least four times compared to the presently working, temporary 100 m high tower. The frequency for the new FM transmitter should be a stand-alone frequency like 100.3 or 107.5 MHz. Short-wave transmitters should be diverted from less important and less-heard foreign services.

Short-Wave Became a Weapon of the Cold War

After the destructive atomic bombing of the Japanese cities of Hiroshima and Nagasaki, the Second World War abruptly came to an end in 1945. The winning major powers were the United States of America, the hard-core capitalistic society and its exact opposite, the Soviet Union, representing Communism. As soon as the war ended, as expected, another war erupted between these two superpowers. Both sides tried to influence as many countries as possible to bring them into their respective camps. This rivalry between the world powers bitterly polarised the planet. Western Europe, Australia, New Zealand, Canada, and Great Britain sided with America. The Soviet Union and its Eastern European allies, which included East Germany, Poland, Romania, Yugoslavia, Albania, Czechoslovakia, Hungary, and some other nations, joined hands to form another formidable grouping. After the Communist takeover, China also, most of the time, sided with the Soviet Union.

There were some big countries like India under Prime Minister Jawahar Lal Nehru, Egypt under President Gamel Abdul Nasser, and Indonesia under President Sukarno, who preferred to stay neutral. However, many African and South American nations were wooed by both groupings. This led to a propaganda war, especially on radio waves. Radio broadcasting was in its infancy during World War I, and medium-wave and long-wave were under different stages of evolution. But during World War II, long-range broadcasting on short-wave became a reality. The BBC wanted to reach every part of the British Empire. However, it was made to compete with Radio Berlin, which had a huge network of short-wave transmitters. To reach India, China, Australia, New Zealand, and Fiji, the BBC had to establish some short-wave transmitters in Kolkata, New Delhi, Mumbai, and Chennai. Naturally, some distortion in the short-wave signal was bound to occur between the British transmission sites and the receiving points in India. More distortion and noisy reception developed during its relay to Southeast Asia and Australia. But, the news did reach the targeted countries.

As far as worldwide short-wave transmission is concerned, the Soviet Union enjoyed a huge advantage over the United States of America due to its enormous landmass. China was easy to cover from the eastern Siberian transmitting sites. Burma, Bangladesh, Nepal, Bhutan, India, Sri Lanka, Pakistan, Afghanistan, Maldives, and Iran could easily be covered from the Radio Moscow short-wave transmitting locations in Tajikistan, Turkmenistan, Uzbekistan, Kazakhstan, Kyrgyzstan, and Azerbaijan. Western Europe could be covered by the Soviet transmitting sites in Russia, Ukraine, and Belarus. African and Middle Eastern countries could also be covered by their super-powered transmitters in Central Asian countries. The North and

South American continents could be covered by high-powered Siberian transmitting stations.

The Voice of America, the mouthpiece of the USA State Department, to counter Soviet propaganda, had to set up its transmitters in the friendly nations of the Philippines, Thailand, Sri Lanka, Greece, England, and a couple of locations in the African continent. The BBC, Radio France International, Australian Broadcasting Corporation (ABC), and the Voice of Germany lent secondary support to the Voice of America. The Cold War is still on, but its intensity has now diminished. After the collapse of the Soviet Union, the Russian financial resources shrunk. This led to the dismantling of the vast network of Radio Moscow, and now it has ceased to exist. Where the Soviet Union has left, China has stepped in. Armed with its newly-acquired prosperity, Radio China International is expanding its operations in most countries. Of course, the USA is its prime target, and India also is its victim of rivalry.

When the BBC Was Alien to Most of America

I lived and worked in the New York-New Jersey area of America for 35 years. The biggest American celebration during the summer happens on 4 July, when the whole nation celebrates America's Independence Day. For the entire year, however, Christmas is the biggest month-long festival. On America's Independence Day, people either gather in their backyards or go to the recreational parks and picnic grounds to do daytime barbecue parties, where all kinds of meat and corn on the cob are grilled.

Around mid-1980s, I attended my first mass-scale Independence Day picnic sponsored by my department. Most of the personnel, from the commissioner down to the summer helps, were in attendance, and they all contributed equally towards the cost of the function. Most of them were carrying something home-cooked to eat and to share with the others. Some of them, especially those from African-American and Hispanic backgrounds, were carrying massive stereo systems with six-to-ten-inch diameter woofers and much smaller tweeters to listen to pop, country, and jazz music. The majority of the picnickers were sharing home-baked cookies and cakes. I also brought a carrot cake loaded with nuts and raisins, which had been baked by my wife. She, too, had accompanied me. Being my first experience with so many unknown people, I experienced a strange feeling that day.

To my surprise, everyone had an AM/FM radio along with a two-cassette tape recording system. I was the only stranger with a world-band tabletop radio in hand. It was one of the first digital radios built by the National/Panasonic Company of Japan. Seeing something strange in my hands, my colleagues and friends surrounded me. My director, Greg Marshall, was curiously looking at this complicated radio. Deputy Director Carl Nordstrom and Administrator John Kraml also showed up at the wooden table that I was sitting at. Several similar tables were provided by the owners of the picnic grounds, and my exotic-looking radio was on display on one of them. I told them that I was going to tune in to the BBC World Service. None believed me. They were wondering how I could tune in to a station located 4,000 miles away. I pulled out my radio's telescopic antenna as much as possible and then tuned in to 7,335 kHz in the 41 m band. The BBC World Service could be heard loud and clear, just like a radio station in the neighbourhood. The accent was non-American. Then some news was read about Glasgow, Aberdeen, Edgbaston, and Manchester. Everyone was surprised to see my magic box.

Later, I did some research on the reasons why short-wave was not a very common listening medium in America. After seeing only AM/FM radios with most Americans, my conclusion was that after the end of World War II, another war, the Cold

War, erupted between the two superpowers, the USA and the USSR. Due to the enormous geographical size of Russia and the Soviet Union, Radio Moscow enjoyed some of the most strategic locations to broadcast most powerfully to the USA and elsewhere in the world. On the other hand, the USA had a smaller land mass, which compelled it to obtain short-wave transmitting sites in a multitude of friendly nations in all parts of the globe. After weighing all the pros and cons, the authorities in the USA, for their population, evolved a policy of encouraging local radio manufacturers and importers from abroad to build only dual-mode AM/FM radios for domestic sales. Moreover, the reproduction of medium-wave and FM sound, by tuning in to local stations, was much better compared to the distantly-located disturbance-prone short-wave. Also, the repair of AM/FM radios was less complicated.

In the subsequent years of my stay in America, the capacity of America's major cable systems, fibre-optic systems and satellite dish networks has increased so much that now we can have easy access to hundreds of channels, including the BBC World Service, Al Jazeera, and some other European and Asian news and entertainment channels. As far as the radio is concerned, most of America still gets AM/FM radios. Nowadays, more powerful radios are also available, but these are outrageously expensive and serve the needs of die-hard short-wave radio enthusiasts only.

My case was different. I had come from India, where short-wave was much more common during the post-World War II period and well up to the 1990s, and where the listeners were hooked to tune in to the BBC, the Voice of America, Radio Ceylon, and other international short-wave services. Before the start of the Internet, listening to All India Radio in America was also my necessity.

Pakistanis Are Eager to Listen to All India Radio

I was in Shoghi, a suburb of Shimla, during the Summer of 2021. Being an ardent radio listener, I took one of my best radio receivers, a German Grundig Satellit 700, as my companion. I could pick up all the Punjab-based AIR stations at this high-altitude location—that, too, quite loud and clear. The most popular programme was a phone-in show of AIR Jalandhar FM Rainbow in the 9–10 a.m. time slot. It was carried simultaneously by the external service radio station AIR Amritsar on 103.6 MHz. The range of the 10-kilowatt FM Rainbow Jalandhar transmitter is 75 km, and due to the low height of the temporary mast, the 20 kW relay transmitter at Gharinda (Amritsar) has reduced range from 100 to a little more than 50 km. However, the Amritsar transmitter, being located close to the Pakistan border, reaches satisfactorily in Lahore and its suburbs. I tried to listen to both stations. The AIR Amritsar transmitter was being blocked by the adjacent frequency 103.7 of AIR Shimla, but the frequency of AIR Jalandhar was a stand-alone frequency 102.7, which was picked up quite well by the listeners in Shimla.

In the phone-in show, Indian listeners make calls from their smartphones, give their locations and phone numbers, and the host of the programme calls them back for a chat. Pakistani listeners are allowed to send voice or written messages. I have heard some very emotional messages from listeners from across the border. This programme is in chaste Punjabi. Punjabi is shunned by the government-owned Radio Pakistan, so they appreciate this pure Punjabi programme more. The Lahori dialect spoken by the Pakistanis is very sweet, and their messages are full of love and affection. Some send their messages from Murree, where this programme has its reach. One particular message came from the Peshawar area. The listener said that this programme did not reach where he lived. So, he used to wake up at 6 a.m. and then walk to a hilltop, which took him one and a half hours. There, he could hear the programme. He enjoyed this programme thoroughly and even sent messages every time he tuned in. This proves how much love they have for the programmes of AIR that are picked up in Pakistan.

One common demand from the Pakistanis is to increase the reach of the programme, which, at present, India cannot. The reason is that the tower designed for this transmitter is a 300 m high structure, which was started in 2006 and completed in 2013 but was not taken over by Prasar Bharati. In 2020, it was partially dismantled to rectify a minor tilt in its upper portion. However, before it could be rebuilt, the Covid-19 pandemic disrupted life. Now, the pandemic is over, but the work of reconstruction has not started, perhaps due to the over-cautious approach of the government. The location is an unpopulated desolate area with no trace of Covid-19. In the absence of a full-height tower, the range is reduced to 25 per cent of its optimum utility range. The Pakistanis are trying to make the best of it, though. Radio Pakistan Lahore is the oldest and the largest radio station in the area. Technically, it is much better administered compared to AIR Jalandhar and the other radio stations in the area. One of the reasons is that no producer or programme executive has been recruited by AIR during the past five years. Hardly any radio station is being administered by an official of the rank of a station director. This has hurt future programming adversely. It appears that the best is behind us.

A Friend in Need

I was living in a small middle-class neighbourhood of 60 homes in the state of New Jersey, which is sandwiched between the megacities of New York and Philadelphia on the eastern seaboard of the United States. Out of these 60 families, 45 were White Europeans, including Egypt's Coptic Christians and Israel's Jewish families. Out of the remainder, there was only one African-American, one Indian Muslim, and one Indian Sikh family. All others were Hindu Indians—mostly from the state of Gujarat, with a business background, and others from the southern peninsular Indian states, with an information technology background.

Most families were headed by white-collar professionals. They all lived in perfect peace and harmony. The neighbours, though, seldom talked to each other. Culturally, even the Whites were poles apart from each other. That is why there were no common social functions where all could harmoniously mingle with each other.

One of my neighbours was an IT professional couple, Mr Chinmay Naimpally and Mrs Sarasvati Naimpally, from Bengaluru, Karnataka. Both had well-paying computer specialist

jobs and two bright kids, both of whom were remarkably good in studies and sports. The Naimpallys were a quiet couple.

America's East Coast is highly prone to hurricanes and tropical storms. Normally, the state of New Jersey does not bear the brunt of tropical storms. The worst wind-gust and rainstorm that my wife and I have ever encountered in America was Hurricane Sandy on the night of 29 October 2012. It resulted in widespread death and destruction, thus spreading misery in almost all the eastern coastal states, the aftermath of which lingered for several days. We had a five-day-long marathon power outage—the worst in my lifetime. The month of October is generally cold in New Jersey, New York, and the New England states. Hence, the misery of the hurricane was exacerbated by the impact of prolonged power failure. We had five harrowing days akin to medieval times; some of the lonely elders were headed into near-depression.

Americans are accustomed to keeping their homes at 70 degrees Fahrenheit (21 degrees Celsius) all year round. But in the absence of electric power, it was impossible to keep the rooms at even ten degrees Celsius. Americans are not accustomed to using heavy quilts either. Even with three blankets, we kept shivering at night. Having come from India, Mr Chinmay was afraid of losing electricity, which is a common occurrence in the country.

To everyone's surprise, he had purchased a diesel generator, which proved extremely useful during that violent storm. It had started with strong howling winds and unstoppable torrential downpours. I was glued to my computer, filing the report about this very storm for *Ajit*, Jalandhar, when the power went down with a big thud. It was pitch dark all around. For some time, nobody moved out of their houses. Some were very scared.

Being a truly good Samaritan, after the rain stopped for a short while, Chinmay Naimpally came out of his home and went from door to door to inform everyone that his generator was available for all to charge their smartphones. He kept his refrigerator and a couple of lights on and could recharge all phones with a multi-outlet plugin for phone charging capability. He could recharge two to three phones at a time. Overnight, the calm and quiet Naimpallys became everyone's favourite couple. Their house remained busy all day. Phone charging continued till midnight, and Sarasvati courageously came to our house to give us back our charged telephones. Suddenly, the Naimpallys became the subject of extraordinary praise from everyone in the neighbourhood. To get the latest storm-related or other information, I kept my transistor radios powered with matching Duracell batteries for emergency information. Several people called me to get the latest storm-related information, and I told them what I knew.

Although all the New York and Philadelphia TV stations were working round the clock, powered by massive diesel generators, no one could see the news on TV due to the blackout. Similarly, all the radio stations were working round the clock, but other than my battery cell-

My radio during Hurricane Sandy—Grundig Radio Satellit 700

operated transistor radios, none could be powered. I gave the latest news to all those who wanted information. After a couple of days, the stuff in the freezers started melting. This led to involuntary ice cream parties. Those who never talked to each other enjoyed different flavours of ice cream like Dairy Queen, Seventh Heaven, and Haagen Dazs at strangers' homes!

Grundig Satellit 700

A young Indian couple, Mr Shreenagesh Bhatkar and Mrs Beena Bhatkar from Goa, also helped everyone. Their home was at a higher elevation and had not been flooded. They offered their helping hand to all who experienced flooding in their basements. In some homes, they drained the water out by using buckets. This noble, time-consuming gesture got them praise from all their white neighbours.

All schools and colleges were closed indefinitely, and all employees on non-essential duties were asked to stay at home. The State Government of New Jersey sent Save Our Souls (SOS) messages to the federal authorities and all the state governments to send all possible help. All the neighbouring states, like Maryland, Virginia, and North Carolina, sent help.

The state of California has as big a heart as its geographic size. It sent nearly complete power grid stations in gigantic C-130 aircraft. States like Illinois and Michigan sent huge amounts of relief material. Pittsburgh area of Pennsylvania helped its big brother, Philadelphia, in its hour of distress. Small, thinly-populated states like Kansas and West Virginia provided a helping hand as well. For a few days, it looked like America was at war with nature and was determined to win at any cost. The Federal Emergency Management Agency was on duty in overdrive. I received all this information through my world-band radio powered by batteries.

Some European Americans had huge quantities of beef and pork products stored in their deep freezers, which had begun to warm up, and the ice had started to melt. They, thus, began to offer their prime beef, seafood, and pork products to everyone. Since meat is a highly sensitive subject in India, I shall not divulge who ate what. After five days of utter misery and helplessness, finally, the mighty power came back, and everyone rushed to the supermarkets to get fresh supplies of eatables—mostly fruits, nuts, and vegetables produced in California. When the East Coast was in deep trouble, California kept its supply chain working. One thing is certain: the Naimpallys and the Bhatkars from far away India, by dint of their outstanding social service, endeared themselves to every household in the neighbourhood.

Most people had at least some part of their roof shingles blown away by the unprecedented wind gusts. Some had their satellite dishes uprooted and windowpanes broken. Even the most miserly insurance companies cooperated beyond normal expectations. After the storm, those who had never talked to their neighbours became good friends.

In Punjab and Haryana, storms of the magnitude of hurricanes seldom occur. The four South Indian peninsular states, plus Odisha, West Bengal, and Maharashtra, do get severe cyclonic storms, but I think America experiences much bigger storms. In winter, the snowstorms (Nor'easters) dumping several feet of snow also hit America hard. I have seen up to three feet deep snow in some parts of New York, Boston, Long Island, and the New England states.

I can unhesitatingly conclude that even in unforeseen and unprecedented crises, Indians can be and shall be the real heroes.

Radio Ceylon: My Favourite

In the latter half of 1950, one day, my father, on his return from the Parliament House, told me that one of his colleagues from the princely state of Mysore, Mr H. Sidhaveerappa, had told him that a new radio station called the Commercial Service in Hindi of Radio Ceylon had popped up on short-wave. The Hindustani music played on this station, according to him, was of very high quality. He, however, being a Kannada, did not have much interest in the Hindustani (Hindi + Urdu) music. My father was aware of my interest in discovering new radio stations. I immediately went up to the radio and tried to locate the new kid on the block. I tried all possible short-wave frequencies but could not find the station. I kept trying for several days without luck.

One day, an acquaintance, Mr Raminder Singh, who was older than me by a dozen years and who served as the Indian military attaché in the country's embassy in Paris and retired as a wing commander in the Indian Air Force, offered to help me in finding the new station. His efforts also failed. So he found the real reason for our repeated failures and bought a ten-foot-long wire from the Connaught Place market. He removed the insulation from half the wire, inserted one end into the jack for the aerial at the back of the radio and hung up the naked side on a wall. It worked, and we could tune in to a host of new radio stations! One fine morning, I found the elusive radio station. The quality of the music was great, but the sound was experiencing dips. K. L. Saigal, Pankaj Mullick, and G. M. Durrani were the frequently heard male voices on this channel. When it came to female voices, the most common were those of Suraiya, Noor Jehan, Amir Bai Karnataki, Zohra Bai of Ambala, and Geeta Roy. The most popular programme was between 7.30 a.m. and 8 a.m. and was dedicated to old film songs. Surprisingly, Lata Mangeshkar's voice was missing. This was when she was a relatively new voice that had been discovered in 1947. This programme continues to date and is quite popular.

After the first general election in 1952, and after attending the lame-duck session, we returned to Kapurthala, where we had a proper rooftop aerial for the radio. Hence, the reception of Radio Ceylon was much better in Kapurthala. My romance with *Purani Filmon Ka Sangeet* (music of old films) continued unabated. *Binaca Geetmala* also started in 1952. Lata Mangeshkar's voice was regularly featured on this programme, as were the voices of Talat Mahmood, Mukesh, Mohammad Rafi, Manna Dey, and Hemant Kumar. Radio Ceylon had good announcers with an excellent choice of music. The lineup included stalwarts like Gopal Sharma, Vijay Kishore Dubey, Manohar Mahajan, Vijay Laxmi, and Dalbir Singh Parmar, just to name a few.

When AIR saw the ground slipping from under its feet, it hurriedly decided to start the Vividh Bharati service. In 1957, Vividh Bharati was recorded in the Bombay studio and aired on short-wave from Mumbai and Chennai. The signal was beamed in the northerly direction. This started giving some competition to Radio Ceylon. However, after the name of the country was changed, the newly-christened Sri Lanka Broadcasting Corporation (SLBC) was sitting prettily over the largest library of film music. It enjoyed a huge advantage over AIR. I kept listening to SLBC Hindi. At one time, *Binaca Geetmala* was the most listened-to one-hour weekly show. SLBC Hindi, though, was my favourite programme, and for decades, it has remained so.

Due to financial difficulties, the short-wave service in Hindi has seen a cut in broadcast time, and the power of the transmitter has been reduced as well. For the past two summers, I have been living in Shimla, where the signal of SLBC Hindi is picked up better. I have been enjoying this great service. The standard of music has not gone down. It appears that the service is frozen in time.

Philips' powerful short-wave and medium-wave radio

The Collapse of the Twin Towers and My Expertise to Help the Government

On the ill-fated morning of 11 September 2001, I was in my office in New Jersey's state capital of Trenton. Suddenly, my secretary, Angela Degliumberto, cried out loudly, 'Oh my God, someone has crashed into the World Trade Centre!' The senior-most secretary in the office, Rose Caravone, could not believe it, but she also started watching the terror attack on the office television. What happened was beyond imagination.

Soon, everyone rushed towards the television, and reality was in front of all. Urgent messages were flashed from the governor's office to most of the offices. That was a day when, for a change, nothing could be accomplished in the office. People were shocked and numb. There was anger all around. As time elapsed, there were demands for retribution. After all, the pride of the only superpower of the world had been severely bruised. All Americans were desperate for a decisive military response.

Only about eight months before this incident, America had sworn in a new President after a bitterly divisive election process. Half the nation had not reconciled to the legitimacy of the election of the new President, George W. Bush Junior. But on that ill-fated day, now known as 9/11, America became one nation under God. This was a blessing in disguise. A shell-shocked and badly fragmented nation became one political monolith. Suddenly, George W. Bush got America's approval. This vicious act of terror eventually led to American intervention in Afghanistan and Iraq.

I was also badly hurt by the events of 9/11. I, too, had a desire to contribute my own two cents for helping America in my humble way. One of the impacts of the plane attack was the coming down of one of America's tallest and biggest radio and television towers, standing at approximately 1,750 ft above the mean sea level. It used to stand, quite majestically, on top of one of America's tallest and grandest twin buildings. The financial loss was worth billions of dollars, but the loss of self-respect was priceless. All of New York's premier television and FM radio channels with a range of 70 miles and more were decimated within minutes. Among those were the most powerful Very High Frequency (VHF) television channels, including channels 4, 5, 7, 9, and 11. In addition, more than a dozen Ultra-High Frequency (UHF) television channels went off the air. The attack killed about 3,000 people, some serving in very senior Wall Street positions—all of them perished in a matter of minutes. A lot more lost limbs and some lost mental equilibrium. With every passing minute, more and more depressing news was being shared on radio and TV.

I wanted to be of some help to America. Although I am a civil engineer with expertise in hydraulics and hydrology, my interests also include long-range sound and picture propagation. What got my attention was the highest mountain peak in New Jersey, within High Point State Park, around 30 miles away from Manhattan. This peak stood at approximately 1,800 ft above the mean sea level. It had a war veterans monument built on top of it, in the shape of an obelisk like the George Washington Monument in Washington D. C. This monument is also on the federal and state lists of heritage landmarks.

I started calculating the FM radio VHF and UHF TV range with a 200-ft-high transmitting mast on the High Point ridge. The calculated range came out to be approximately 75 miles all around, which is more than the range of the World Trade Centre mast. If approved, this mast could have covered almost as much area and population as the terror-destroyed World Trade Centre mast. This mast could have been fabricated in about two months with the technology and expertise available in America. There were several construction companies capable of rapid construction of tall steel or concrete towers in metropolitan New York.

Once the calculations were finished, I wanted to share my concept with the public in the worst-impacted tri-state area. I talked to my colleagues within my department, who advised me against moving ahead with my proposal because the High Point Monument was a federally protected historic landmark, and obtaining permission for any construction within its vicinity would have been an uphill task. Like a stubborn child, though, I was bent on preparing and sharing my report. The authorisation to publish the proposal would have to come from at least an officer of the level of a divisional director, which is somewhat equivalent to a deputy minister in an Indian state. I went straight to my director in his front office. I discussed it with him. A very helpful director, Greg Marshall, personally liked the idea. He told me that his permission stands granted, but he warned me that all the lovers of heritage would pounce on me. So, if I could have thick enough skin to bear all the abuses and rebukes, I was permitted to publish it. Another very senior officer, John Garcia, advised me against inviting unnecessary trouble. However, I was adamant about taking the chance.

I sent my report to *The Trenton Times*, a daily that was published from New Jersey's state capital. To my utter surprise, the newspaper carried it prominently on the 'Op-Ed' page within two days of my posting. As expected, all the heritage lovers in New Jersey were up in arms against my proposal, and I was made to suffer severe criticism, but I received a lot of support from several unexpected quarters, including the conservatives and liberals. For several days, I kept receiving bouquets and brickbats from known and unknown folks.

The final decision about the building of the World Trade Centre was to be taken at the highest federal, state, and New York City levels. The eventual decision, after years of brainstorming, was taken to rebuild the entire destroyed cluster of buildings in the same area, including the construction of the multi-channel broadcasting tower. The largest twin buildings were to be replaced by a single, even bigger and taller building. It was to be a modern engineering marvel. That is how it was during those tumultuous days in American history.

Medium-Wave in India

The oldest radio broadcasting spectrum in use all over the world, in the common man's language, is called a medium-wave. In America, the commonly used word for medium-wave is AM, which is a scientific name for medium-wave, long-wave, and short-wave sound propagation. When radio took birth in Europe and America in the early 1920s, it used a wavelength spectrum roughly spread from 200–500 m. All the earliest established radio stations in the United States of America, from Pittsburgh (Pennsylvania) to New York, Boston, Philadelphia, San Francisco, Los Angeles, Chicago, and Detroit, had used frequencies from 1,500 kilocycles per second to 600 kilocycles per second, which corresponded with 200–500 m in wavelength. The need for long-hop short-wave service arose during World War II, between 1939 and 1945, when the British and the Germans wanted to reach faraway countries with their version of war news. After World War II, short-wave assumed the role of the primary weapon of the Cold War between the post-1945 Soviet Union and the United States.

Medium-wave has the unique characteristic of bending the waves in accordance with the topography of the land within its coverage range. It propagates its signal in ground waves as well as the sky waves over land, mountains, and oceans. The sunlight absorbs the sky waves as long as it shines during the daylight hours, but at night, the sky waves travel unhindered, sometimes from 10 times to 20 times beyond their daytime range, depending on the weather and prevailing atmospheric conditions, but the quality of signal deteriorates as it attenuates at night. The range of a medium-wave transmitter is calculated based on the reach of its ground waves, which, in turn, is determined during daylight hours. The nightly range of amplitude modulation (medium-wave) is unpredictable and, hence, is ignored. In America, in the case of high-powered transmitters, the operation at night is regulated. In some cases, it is disallowed.

America has made the most extensive uninterrupted use of medium-wave for nearly 100 years. It is still in active use from coast to coast and from the Canadian border to the Mexican border. There are more than 1,000 medium-wave radio stations active in the United States. Of course, FM ensures the state-of-the-art quality of sound, unaffected by the vagaries of weather, but its range is the shortest. The advanced nations have stretched the FM usage as much as they could, but they never tried to completely retire the old workhorse—the medium-wave spectrum. Now, the medium-wave is not used for serious listening to music and is used for news broadcasts and talk shows. It is used by big corporations and community organisations alike. The evangelists in America are allowed to use both medium-wave and short-wave. I can understand the pros and cons of all the systems, but I fail to understand the tearing hurry in India to discard medium-waves altogether. The large states where, at one time, more than a dozen medium-wave transmitters were in operation are now left with merely one or two medium-wave transmitters. Take the case of Uttar Pradesh, where at one time Lucknow, Allahabad, Varanasi, Mathura, Vrindavan, Gorakhpur, Rampur, and Najibabad had more than 12 medium-wave transmitters, now have replaced most medium-wave transmitters with FM transmitters. In addition, places like Raebareli and Amethi have high-powered FM transmitters installed on expensive high-mast towers.

One reason for the slow death of medium-wave in India is the opening of only the FM spectrum to private-sector corporate houses. These corporations have the influence and means to discourage the manufacture of certain kinds of merchandise. For example, they can stop the manufacture of medium-wave radio receivers because they do not use them. To get over this tendency, the private sector should be allowed to use medium-wave frequencies for their radio stations. A lot of them will opt for more affordable medium-wave stations in smaller towns and villages, where FM is not affordable.

In America, both FM and medium-wave are used by the private sector. For example, in New York, CBS, which is a big corporation, uses 880 kHz in the medium-wave band for their all-news radio station with the call sign WCBS. Similarly, the American Broadcasting Corporation (ABC) uses 770 kHz for its biggest radio station in New York. The NBC is using high-powered medium-wave stations too.

India should also go back to the pre-1970s 10 kHz station separation, which was more convenient and could ensure a slightly better quality of sound due to more bandwidth. I fail to understand why India subjugated itself to 9 kHz station separation on medium-wave, whereas America stubbornly stuck to the old 10 kHz separation. America has also gone below

540 kHz and 530 kHz for some of its radio stations. On the upper side, America has been seen using frequencies up to 1,680 kHz. This expansion gives America several more frequencies in the medium-wave band. I strongly feel that India should not abandon medium-wave, at least as long as the other nations are using it. India is a vast country with a high-density population and numerous ethnic and linguistic groups. Why should it overburden the FM spectrum and abandon a complete broadcast spectrum, which it has been using extensively since the inception of broadcasting until recently?

In hilly terrains, in some cases, the tall mountain ranges extensively obstruct the FM signals. Medium-waves can offer an easy escape from such situations. I fail to understand why present-day India is mindlessly shutting the door on this viable option. Scientific improvements are taking place all the time to improve the quality of reception of medium-wave radio signals in Europe and the Americas. India can certainly make use of all these technical innovations for its new generation of medium-wave transmitters.

Pakistan is still using medium-waves extensively, especially for targeting India. Their major stations in Karachi, Quetta, Peshawar, Islamabad, and Lahore all have high-powered medium-wave transmitters. They target the Amritsar region on medium-waves. We can also rely on medium-wave and FM. Our border FM radio station in Amritsar, after its completion, will have more range than any FM station in Pakistan. We should complete it quickly and supplement it with a 300-kW medium-wave transmitter. Land for a medium-wave transmitter is available at the FM site. My advice to Prasar Bharati is to not abandon the use of medium-waves.

Manohar Singh Gill and the DD

This is a true story of the time after the 'National Emergency of India 1975–1977'. After the 1977 parliamentary elections, the country was ruled by Prime Minister Morarji Desai of the newly cobbled together Janata Party and in Punjab, Sardar Parkash Singh Badal of the Shiromani Akali Dal was serving his second term as the Chief Minister. Television was new to Punjab. One television station had already been functioning since 1973 in Amritsar, and the second, a much bigger one meant for a capital station, was in an advanced stage of construction. The studio complex was already functioning on the famous Bhagwan Mahavir Marg in a posh area of Jullundur (now Jalandhar) city, and a magnificent reinforced cement concrete tower was in an advanced stage of construction in a nearby village called Khurla Kingra.

Black and white television receivers with bulky picture tubes were selling like hotcakes, and demand was outstripping the supply. Manufacturing of television receivers was concentrated in New Delhi and the then city of Bombay. One daredevil industrialist of Punjab, Sardar H. S. Bhatti, opened an assembling unit for television receivers in Mohali. For the formal inauguration of the factory, he invited Shri Inder Kumar Gujral, a highly respected politician originally hailing from district Jhelum in Rawalpindi division of West Punjab. An obviously knowledgeable Mr Gujral started talking about the rags-to-riches Punjabis, who came to East Punjab as paupers, but by dint of their hard work, they turned the corner and developed deep pockets. The Punjabis had money, and they were willing to spend it on luxurious items. Gujral Sahib said that he plans to cover every part of the state with low-height and low-powered television transmitters by building about thirty repeater stations. I was listening to Mr Gujral. According to my engineering common sense, Punjab had two high hills located to its North, from where a distance of up to 100 miles in radius could be covered by locating 10 kW or more powerful transmitters.

When the function was over, and the guests were served tea and snacks, I talked to Mr Gujral and told him that Punjab would soon have two television stations along with studios and two more at Kasauli and Dalhousie could cover 80 per cent of the geographical area of the state; we would need only one more transmitter in the Bathinda-Abohar belt to cover the entire state. He was happy to hear that. During those days, security was not a concern, and VIPs could mingle freely with ordinary people.

Sardar Manohar Singh Gill, who was the Principal Secretary attached to the Chief Minister then, overheard our conversation. He had a piece of advice for me. He told me that rather than writing independently to the central government, I should route my suggestion through the Chief Minister. He told me to go home and get down to my drawing board, make a draft of the letter and bring it to him. He would modify and return it to me to type the final letter and submit it for the Chief Minister's signatures. The same was done. The Chief Minister not only got appreciation from the centre, but Punjab received the gift of a magnificent-looking broadcasting tower at Kasauli in neighbouring Himachal Pradesh. Initially, it carried the services of Doordarshan Jalandhar and Doordarshan National based in New Delhi. Later on, when FM came, the AIR Chandigarh 107.2 MHz and AIR Jalandhar Primary Channel 100.9 MHz were installed on this tower. This was one of the several ways of getting things done that Dr. Manohar Singh Gill used in his long career as a top bureaucrat in India. Later on, he served as one of the Election Commissioners of India and subsequently as the Chief Election Commissioner of India. Later, he served as a two-term member of the Rajya Sabha and as a union minister. He died at the age of 87 on 15th October 2023. He was born on 14th June 1936.

Part-III

MUSINGS

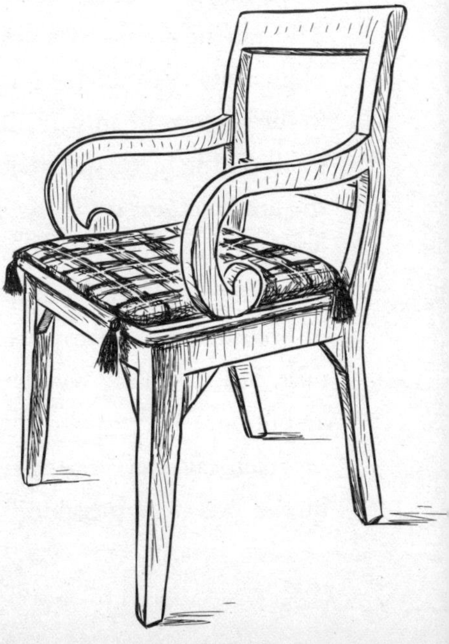

Teaching by Visual Demonstration

In 1968, I was selected to serve at the Punjab Engineering College (PEC) as a teacher in the civil engineering department. Normally, new teachers are not asked to choose their teaching subject, but I was specifically asked by my Head of Department, Professor R. C. Sharma, to express my preference for the subject to be taught. During those days, Mr Himmat Singh Chadha, who taught architecture and town planning, was going to the United States for higher studies, and I had developed an interest in the subject. I had studied Bannister Fletchure's most popular book on the history of architecture and so had a good grasp of the architectural styles of Frank Lloyd Wright and some other modern architects. Of course, Le Corbusier's town planning was at my fingertips. Without hesitation, I opted to teach the subject of architecture and town planning. It was quite a challenging task, but it was my own choice; running away from it was not an option.

From day one, I started evolving a plan for teaching my subject in the best way possible. I knew all along that when Indian engineering graduates go abroad, their major qualification is their theoretical knowledge, and their major drawback is their lack of practical experience. Hence, I tried to evolve a solution to conquer this drawback. There was a provision for an all-India tour for the students of the final year or the third year, and considering the weather in Chandigarh, the month of December was the most suitable for undertaking this tour, which would not exceed a month in total duration. Usually, during this month, Chandigarh is very cold, but the rest of India, which was to be toured, is less cold, and some places like Mumbai and Chennai are outright warm. I knew that this would be the best month for an all-India tour. I chose the appropriate places to demonstrate the best specimens of architecture in India. We were a group of three teachers, and all of us chose places of our teaching interest for the tour. I led two all-India tours. The first was in December 1968. It lasted for less than one month. The second was in the same month in 1969, and it lasted for a month. We had to slug it out with the Northern Railway authorities to get a new economy-class coach, which was attached to long-distance trains. Generally, a group of 50 students took the tour each year. They were all accommodated into one coach. We started from Chandigarh, and the first stop was in Lucknow, where we visited the Bara Imambara, the Chhota Imambara, and the Roomi Darwaza—three specimens of Islamic architecture. We also visited the ruins of the once magnificent Residency in Lucknow. Our stay in Lucknow lasted for two days, enough to study Islamic architecture in northern India.

The next stop was in Kolkata, the largest metropolis of India during those days. The stay there lasted for three days. The most impressive building we visited was the Victoria Memorial, a specimen of early twentieth-century British architectural revival.

Some other buildings we saw were the docks in the port area and the West Bengal Civil Secretariat building. The Howrah Bridge was a specimen of a balanced cantilever bridge technology, but it looked very similar to a suspension bridge. We took the help of a railway engineer to understand its engineering design. The Howrah Railway Station looked like the Paddington Junction Railway Station in London. It is the largest railway station in India. The British built it more than 100 years ago, and it was, and still is, handling the traffic. To broaden the outlook of the students, we made a trip to the Indian Museum, which, during those days, used to be the best museum in India. Then, there was the National Museum in New Delhi, which was still being equipped. To our amazement, the tram service was still successful in Kolkata! Its frequency was one tram every 30 seconds. Kolkata was the first city on our tour, where London-style double-decker buses were plying on busy routes like Chowringhee Bazar and Park Street.

Our next stop was Chennai, which was warm, like May in Punjab. We travelled all night on an express train to reach Chennai, starting from Kolkata. India's largest and oldest rail coach factory was located near Chennai. The one in Kapurthala was built long after this, in 1986. Being a port city in southern peninsular India, it had several large factories, including the Ashok Leyland bus and truck manufacturing factory.

We spent two days in Chennai and reached Bengaluru on an overnight journey. The latter's weather was warmer than Chandigarh's. It was a place of modern engineering science. The IT revolution of Bengaluru came about much later. Its telephone company, Bharat Electronic Limited (BEL), was the most advanced in India at that time. Mysore, located next door, was a big centre of southern India's Hindu Dravidian architecture. Its royal palace was an engineering masterpiece of British structural design and the architectural style of the Karnataka region. Some students wanted to visit Goa, but there was not much engineering information to be seen there. So, we persuaded the boys to skip it.

In 1968, we skipped Hyderabad, but in 1969, Hyderabad was prominent on the itinerary. For a change, we saw the Salar Jung Museum and Char Minar. The IT industry was in its infancy then.

Mumbai was the next stop. Its biggest railway station, then known as the Victoria Terminus (now renamed to the Chhatrapati Shivaji Terminus), was the station where our rented coach was parked. First, we studied its magnificent architecture. The Fort Area, Flora Fountain, and Colaba, located nearby, were the most magnificent specimens of British architecture. The Taj Mahal Palace, Mumbai, is the most magnificent five-star hotel in the city. Perhaps so, in the whole of India. We saw the picturesque Marine Drive and Malabar Hill as well. The largest sewerage treatment plant in Mumbai was also the easiest to study. The famous Electric Railway System of Mumbai was the first mass transit system of India, and we studied it by travelling in the jam-packed local transit system! Most students wanted to see some of the famous film studios of Bollywood. Here, the teaching staff had to give in. Luckily, there was no dispute between the tour officials and the students during both tours. I was in the group that watched a live recording session of the Melody Queen of India—Lata Mangeshkar.

After Mumbai, we saw the Ajanta and Ellora caves as specimens of ancient Hindu and Buddhist architecture.

Our last stops were at Agra and Fatehpur Sikri, where we studied the town planning and architecture of the Mughal era and New Delhi, where all the architectural styles blended. We saw Edward Lutyen's Raisina Hill, where the Rashtrapati Bhawan (previously, Viceregal Lodge or the Government House), North and South Blocks of the Central Secretariat, the Parliament House, and the India Gate are located. Connaught Place was New Delhi's most fashionable business district. There were old Hindu temples, Sikh gurdwaras, Jama Masjid, and the Red Fort too. We visited all these sites plus a lot more. This is the way it was more than half a century ago. Most educational tours end in friction between the faculty and the students, but we managed by accommodating each other's concerns.

American and Indian Democracy

India claims to be the world's largest democracy. Based on the country's massive population of 1,400 million, which is the second highest in the world after Communist China, India's claim appears justified. America, on the other hand, claims to be the oldest and the second-biggest democracy in the world. America's claim is also just. Otherwise, in the real sense of the word, both democracies are flawed, and both need drastic alterations to be in sync with the modern-day needs and realities of democracy. America claims itself as the oldest democracy in the world, but for more than 50 years, it did not bestow voting rights on its countless African Americans until the Civil War, started by President Abraham Lincoln, gave voting rights to the millions of sons and daughters of the once-upon-a-time African slaves. The American claim is technically correct because the Americans have been holding democratic elections since the declaration of its independence from Great Britain on 4 July 1776 in the city of Philadelphia in the sprawling Commonwealth of Pennsylvania. From day one, the United States of America has been predominantly a Christian country, with more than 80 per cent of its population believing in Jesus Christ.

On the other hand, India is an ancient, predominantly Hindu society with more than 75 per cent Hindu population. Whereas the minority groups in America are much smaller, ranging between 0.7 million Sikhs to one million Buddhists, two million Hindus, three million Jews, and eight million Muslims, the population of Muslims, by themselves, in India is estimated between 20–30 per cent. As of this moment, on paper, both countries give equal rights to their minorities, but practically the biggest minorities are unhappy, and the majority are feeling threatened by the runaway growth of major minorities, especially the followers of Islam. In a way, both countries are sitting on a volcano of communal and racial hatred. The biggest test for both democracies is to keep their majority-minority relations under check. The beauty of democracy lies in its need-based evolution. Let us see how both democracies will evolve to solve their racial and communal problems, along with the growing intolerance with the rising numbers of minorities.

Every state and the Union Government of India holds its elections once every five years at the same time or at different times unless any of its governments collapses without completing its full term, and the possibility of formation of a legitimate alternative government appears unreal. India's emphatic claim of being the largest democracy in the world is also perfectly right. India has a tradition of governing the states through the institution of unelected and centrally-appointed governors, who *de facto* serve as the agents of the central authorities. Whenever there are opposing parties ruling at the centre and the state, the conflict between the governor and the state's elected leadership takes an ugly, undemocratic turn. The governors are known to impose the will of the centre on the states by disregarding the concerns of the states. This is against the principles of true federalism. Such scenarios make the Indian democracy seem like an unequal clash between the mighty centre and the disadvantaged states, in which, most of the time, the centre emerges victorious, thus inflicting chronic wounds on the rights and privileges of the states. The simmering discontentment poses a big threat to the not-so-old Indian democracy.

America believes in a strong, not easily violable, federal set-up. There is a clear demarcation of powers between the federal and the state governments. The federal authority often shuns blatant encroachment on the powers delegated to the tiniest of states. This restricts federal and state conflicts to a minimum. In the event of a federal and state conflict, the Federal Supreme Court adjudicates. But lately, serious doubts have been raised about the neutrality of the United States Supreme Court. The genesis of the problem appears in the process of appointment of judges. American judges are appointed not by a process of judicial scrutiny but by the American presidents. Also, there is a suspicion that the appointed judges toe the line of their appointing authorities and their parties. According to some critics in the present day, in the Supreme Court, out of a total of nine judges, six are Republicans, and three are Democratic appointees. Whom, then, does one trust when even the Supreme Court is considered partisan? This is the worst flaw of the US judiciary.

Just like the European nations, America is a country with a preponderance of Christian population. Here, Christianity dominates in the form of oaths taken to perform the duties of elected offices that they will hold. Thus, Christianity becomes an essential part of the day-to-day life of even the non-Christian population. The major minority in the USA, especially the Muslims, sometimes feel suffocated. They feel the system is inadvertently not letting minorities live their lives in their way or let their grievances be heard at the legal and administrative levels properly.

When India attained its independence from Great Britain and got down to deliberating the nitty-gritty of its constitution, it conceived secular plurality as the essence of its constitution. But, over the years, big flaws have surfaced in the implementation of the Indian Constitution, which, according to the thinkers in the West, are not letting India attain the status it aspires for, even in the United Nations. These are rights that India has been demanding from the United Nations for decades. For example, India is engaged in perpetual back-channel negotiations to get a permanent seat in the United Nations Security Council, with the power to veto proposals that are unacceptable to India. Most of the nations do not appear to be opposed to India, at least this is what they publicly profess, but when it comes to voting for permanent membership of the Security Council, all nations with the power to veto line up against India and the result, invariably, goes against India. Therefore, Indian diplomacy has failed in the United Nations, and the much-needed expansion of the UN Security Council has not taken place. The Indian democracy appears to be a loser in the community of nations. There is a perception that, at present, the Muslim population in India is feeling ill at ease with the way the government is treating the Muslims of the republic.

One of the biggest strengths of the American way of conducting its periodic elections is its counting of votes immediately after the completion of polling. In some of the states where electronic voting occurs, some of the results pour out immediately after polls are closed. Some of the presidential results of polling start to appear within minutes of the closing of voting. This increases the legitimacy of the polling process. Even in the largest states, the election results come quickly.

In this matter, India's record of the entire polling process is, at best, poor. India still appears to be stuck in a colonial mindset, which is not even close to democratic practices. We have an all-powerful election commission in India, which dictates the timetable of every big or small election process. Polling is controlled from the start of the polling timetable to its culmination. All the electronic polling machines are then sealed and kept under lock and key for several days. After the prolonged storage under police protection, the electronic voting machines are retrieved and opened, and counting is carried out at a painfully slow pace. Each electoral counting exercise goes into numerous rounds, and results keep evolving. Every counting process goes on for several hours, and when completed, it gets submitted to the higher authorities. This cumbersome process results in an agonising waste of time. Due to suspicion at every stage of the election process, public faith in the exercise of polling takes a severe beating.

Almost all political parties in India are completely subjugated to the autocratic party presidents who wield dictatorial powers. The working committees are merely their rubber stamps. Tickets to contest the elections are awarded arbitrarily by the party presidents or conveners and their cronies. In America, there is a system of holding primaries. Whosoever is chosen in the primaries, through popular votes, gets the right to contest the election. Due to this, the most deserving candidate gets the right to represent the party in their constituency.

America is also divided by the level of education of its voters. There are a majority of predominantly agricultural states, where most of the people possess no college education. These states have the least number of international airports, and most of these people have not travelled beyond the American land border. They work hard five days a week. On Sundays, everyone visits churches, and at the time of voting, they all listen to their priests. They are mostly conservatives, and in their states, most of the time, the Republicans win.

There are some coastal states with lots of international airports for worldwide mobility in the areas where they serve. This widens the outlook of people. They have a higher percentage of college graduates. They have a much bigger percentage of minorities, most of them being from the African-American community. These states, at one time, were highly industrialised. Now, they are known as the Rust Belt states. They generally vote for the Democratic Party candidates. This is how the nation is fragmented. The west coastal states, the northern Rust Belt, and the upper-eastern seaboard states fall into this category. They generally vote for the Democratic Party.

Most of the states in the southern Sun Belt region and the potbelly agricultural Mid-West region are staunch supporters of the Republican Party. The election results in most of these states are invariably foregone conclusions—they rarely spring a surprise. There are other states, though, where the composition of the population keeps changing. The results in these states also keep changing with the alterations in the population demographics. For example, in the largest state of California, the population of Mexican Hispanics is rising all the time. The election results reflect the impact of population changes. Most Mexicans support the Democrats, and so does California as the state.

Similarly, in New York, the changes in immigration patterns are reflected in the election results. Some long-time, white-populated constituencies are now changing. The new arrivals are either information technology experts from India or domestic help workers from Puerto Rico, Mexico, Bangladesh, Guatemala, Venezuela, or other less-affluent nations. Some technical hands from the Islamic nations are also joining the labour force in New York. When they become citizens of America in the states of New York, New Jersey, and the neighbouring New England states, they do impact the results. It has been seen that the states of New York and New Jersey are turning Democratic.

There was a slightly Republican-leaning twelfth US House of Representatives district in New Jersey. It consisted of Somerset County and its surroundings. During the 1990s, New Jersey was slightly leaning towards the Democratic Party, but it had only 12 electoral districts. The Democrats used to win all their districts with comfortable margins. On the other hand, the Republicans used to win in tight races. The twelfth district used to witness the closest fight. The margin of Republican victory in this constituency was generally less than 1,000 votes. The Democrats could flip it, but they needed to bring every possible vote to the polling booth. The voting population of this well-off constituency consisted of about 70 per cent Whites, about 20 per cent African-Americans, and the remaining 10 per cent were Hindus, Muslims, Sikhs, and Chinese. I am counting the Jewish voters with the Whites.

Gurdwara Bridgewater is the oldest gurdwara in the state of New Jersey. Most of the time, I used to serve as the secretary every alternate year. Occasionally, I served as the President, too. On one Sunday morning in August 1998, I was conducting the stage. A thinly-built, tall, white, handsome man showed up at the entrance door of the gurdwara. He was desirous of addressing the Sunday congregation. He introduced himself as Rush Holt, a scientist by profession but serving as a politician. He told us that he had won the Democratic Primary election from his twelfth electoral district and was contesting the seat for the US House of Representatives on behalf of his party. I allowed him to speak to the audience. His speech was impressive and convincing.

From left to right:
Jon Corzine, incumbent Governor; author Harjap Singh Aujla; Rush Holt, Member of the US House of Representatives; and Jim McGreary, former Governor.

In the end, he asked me if he could win. I told him that this congregation could deliver at most 300 votes, which would be insufficient for his victory. Then I told him that he must go to the South Indian Hindu temple located nearby and make a request for votes. I asked him to place his fliers in the largest Asian-Indian market on Oak Tree Road in the townships of Edison and Iselin. He did all that. I asked him to show up in all the mosques in his constituency. He did that, too. His constituency saw brisk polling. Counting started at 8 p.m. on the same evening. Till about midnight, he was trailing. Considering him defeated, I went to bed. At around one in the morning, I received a call from a friend telling me that Rush Holt had won! Then, we visited his election headquarters. Celebrations were on. We were received with open arms. A sure defeat had turned into a narrow victory. After that, he used the same formula to win many more close elections.

The IT expert immigrants from Bengaluru, Hyderabad, Pune, Mumbai, Gurgaon, and other Indian cities are becoming American citizens, and they are instrumental in several Democratic victories in America, including in New York, New Jersey, and California.

Trump is blowing his own trumpet to corrupt the American democratic system. American democracy designates a lot of power to the President of the United States. This democracy was not prepared for an autocratic, and in fact, an almost fascist leader who would use the system for his personal selfish reasons, especially one who idolises dictators like Vladimir Putin of Russia and Kim Jong-Un of North Korea and wants to emulate them. He tried to use the majority community in America for his selfish electoral aims. His main followers are extreme right-wing Republicans who idolise him. In the 2016 presidential elections, he was pitted against Hillary Clinton, the Democratic nominee. In the overall vote count, Hillary won by approximately three million votes. However, America's skewed electoral college system gave the victory to Trump. For four years, he misused the system to the hilt for his gains and the gains of the super-rich class. His bluff was called out in the 2020 elections, and his older rival, Joe Biden, defeated him in a landslide victory. That was when Trump tried his utmost to discredit the election results and declare himself the winner of the presidency of America. He filed multiple lawsuits to overturn the results of the legitimately held election, but they all failed, and some harsh judgements came from his own appointee judges. His own President and other top officials in his cabinet accused him, saying that he had lost the election but did not care. Then, there was the insurrection at Capitol Hill on 6 January 2021, which had been instigated by him and his cronies. This resulted in the loss of life and limb. Several vital federal documents were destroyed, and Capitol Hill was damaged as well. He, to this day, denies the results of the popular verdict. In the midterm elections of 2022, his party was expected to make substantial gains, but it miserably failed to do so.

He intends to contest the 2024 presidential election all over again and has already announced his candidature. The popular winners of his party have realised that Trump is a liability and that he should not contest the election. They think he has enough votes within the Republican Party to win his and his cronies' nomination, and no one else would be nominated in the primaries without his tacit approval. But, after being nominated, his candidates will not have enough votes among the independent voters to get elected in the nationwide elections. Therefore, his party will fall short of a majority in the Senate.

His party's narrow victory in the election to the House of Representatives in 2022 does not give them enough power. The razor-thin victory makes the party a lame-duck majority. If the Republican Party must save itself from permanent doom, then it should modify its policies to guarantee the rights of women and other groups whose votes are vital for winning. On the other hand, the Democratic Party has learnt to become an all-inclusive party. They target minority votes plus the votes from the majority community.

Of late, the Republican Party of America has mastered the art of gerrymandering the constituencies with sizeable minority votes. Every ten years, the electoral constituencies can be redrawn where the majority community (in America, it is the community of European Whites, who are leaning towards the Republican Party) gerrymanders to ensure their victory in the elections. It packs most of the minority community population in a small number of electoral districts. An average electoral district should normally be a compact geographical district, but under gerrymandering, most of the African-American populated areas are combined to make a linear or zigzag-shaped constituency, where they have an 80–90 per cent majority. These areas elect African-American (mostly Democratic Party) candidates with landslide margins. In other areas, the majority community wins with slimmer margins in more districts. This type of gerrymandering has been done in most of the potbelly agricultural midwestern states and the southern coastal Sun Belt states of America. This practice results in unfair electoral results, which are contrary to legitimate Democratic principles. It is heartening to note that there is no such thing in the Indian democracy.

India must be careful to avoid the pitfalls that the Republican Party in America is facing these days. India is, by and large, a poor country whose policies must not abandon the have-nots. India and America are two democracies with a vast disparity in income levels. India should also avoid giving away freebies to its electorate, which is detrimental to the health of the national and state exchequers. As America has been caught in the web of covert racism, India should not fall into the trap of communalism. India has a constitution which guarantees equal rights to minorities and is considered a secular republic. It sits in the middle of a sea of parochial Islam. However, now, India seems to be falling into the trap of rule by the plurality of the majority community against the interest of the minorities. It is a nation of diverse cultures and ethnic groups and can ill afford to follow the path of communalism. Hence, it should focus on its development by ensuring equal rights for all.

Indian Jugad for an American Problem

When I was serving the Government of New Jersey as a civil engineer during the 1990s, my administrator, John Kraml, gave me a ticklish problem that no one else was willing to handle. During the 1840s and 1850s, several railroad lines had been constructed all over the industrial coastal and northern industrial America. One of those lines was the Sussex Valley Railroad. When automobiles, like cars, proliferated in America, some of these railroad lines became financially unviable and had to be abandoned. The Sussex Line was considered uneconomical and was dismantled. The steel rails were removed, but the timber sleepers were left to rot *in situ*. Although the rail lines were gone, the bridges over the running brooks and dry water courses were not removed. These bridges were built for heavy goods traffic. The government wanted to use the right side of the abandoned railroad line to make walking, jogging, and bicycle-riding trails for common people. I was asked to evaluate the load-carrying capacities of all the bridges so that no mishaps would occur. It was an uphill task, which would have taken years to analyse had conventional methods been used.

I covered the entire length on foot, which took me more than a week. I photographed all the bridges and took the measurements of all the steel sections used. I visually examined the piers and abutments. All the steel members, being 150 years old, were severely rusted. It was rather impossible to evaluate their load-carrying capacity. I did not want to give up without exhausting all my options. Looking for a quick fix, I went to the design office of the New Jersey Department of Transportation, where a friend of mine, Mr Rajinder Pal Singh Chawla, was a supervising engineer. He was very helpful and innovative; I was sure he would be of great help. Had I gone to anyone unknown, I would have faced a barrage of questions.

I explained my predicament and asked him if he had a solution in mind. He looked at the pictures and found them to be familiar with some of the railroad bridges that he had analysed on the main design office computer system. He asked me to subtract 25 per cent of the cross-sectional area of the load-bearing members because of rust but to keep the dead load unchanged and feed the data into the computer. I did exactly that. He then asked me to wait a bit. The computer hesitated initially and then started churning out the report. The first results were encouraging. One by one, I fed the data of every bridge and got the results for about a dozen bridges. According to the results, the load-bearing capacity of each bridge, in layman's terms, was less than that of a freight wagon but adequate for a passenger coach. We were putting very light traffic. My purpose was served. All the bridges were fully capable of handling loads of motorcycles, Bobcat maintenance vehicles, and departmental vehicles. I prepared, signed, and submitted the report to my higher authorities, and after their approval, the way was cleared for converting the entire length of the erstwhile railroad line into a walking and jogging trail. All that we had to do was replace the wooden sleepers on the bridges, put a brand-new decking made from Canadian lumber, and stain it for longer life. Horse riders were allowed to use the trail, provided they physically removed the excreta of their horses. For lovers of nature, this trail is now very popular. This is how an Indian *jugad* worked in American conditions. For me, Mr Rajinder Pal Singh Chawla is an unsung hero.

The Lull Before the Internet Storm

Let's talk about the United States of the early 1980s when work was underway for what is now called the World Wide Web and its multitude of offshoots like Facebook, YouTube, WhatsApp, Twitter, and e-mails. In 1980, a very compassionate groundnut-growing farmer, Jimmy Carter, was the President of the United States of America. He was a gentleman to the core. During this time, an unreasonable firebrand, Shiite Islamic religious heavyweight, Ayatollah Ruhollah Khomeini, had—after overthrowing the secular and progressive government of the Shah of Iran—assumed the *de facto* sole politico-religious leadership of Iran.

In an unprecedented action in the history of nations, Ayatollah Khomeini ordered the taking over of hostages of the entire staff of the Embassy of the United States in Tehran. A peace-loving Jimmy Carter wanted to negotiate a gentlemanly solution to resolve the hostage problem. He could afford to take destructive military action to rescue all the hostages, but he wanted to avoid a bloodbath and collateral damage, which was inevitable while conducting ruthless dictatorial actions. His wavering resolve became his undoing, and he was defeated in the general election of November 1980 by a flamboyant actor-turned-politician, Ronald Reagan, a nominee of the extreme right-winger Republican Party.

In Afghanistan, the Soviet Union contemplated a military action with disastrous results in 1979. In February 1980, the colourful Winter Olympics were held in the frigid upstate New York. In addition to other surprising sporting successes, the Americans annexed the coveted ice hockey gold medal, defeating the much-fancied, top-favoured team of the Soviet Union. The triumphant Americans were in a euphoric celebratory mode from coast to coast.

The 1980 Summer Olympiad was hosted by America's Cold War rivals, the Soviet Union, in Moscow. A highly-conceited America did not accord due respect to the biggest sports carnival in the world. Even the coverage of field hockey matches was treated as a listless affair within America. I had to take three hours off from my work to try to watch the final match between India and Spain on television or hear it on the radio. Whereas the most high-tech American television disappointed me thoroughly, the BBC World Service on radio prominently gave the scores, and the result was three goals by India versus two goals by Spain. Thus, India won the men's field hockey gold medal for the record eighth time. This was to be the last time to date, though. This is an unbeaten Olympic record. For the rest of the day, I was most upbeat in the office, too. The evening was a time for all Indians to begin celebrating, and we did it by cutting a cake.

I found out, most painfully, that America is a self-centred nation. One thing that I missed badly in America was the fresh daily dose of news from India. America had some India-centric English language newspapers published from New York, Chicago, and the western coastal cities of San Francisco and Los Angeles, which collected news every day from India and published it on the weekends. I was better informed than the India-centric newspapers. On my powerful digital short-wave National Panasonic radio, RF-2900, I could listen to the General Overseas Service of AIR directed towards the United Kingdom, which did not give the domestic news in its entirety, but I used to get most of the important news, nevertheless.

The Republican presidential hopeful, Ronald Reagan, registered an emphatic landslide victory in the 1980 general election held on the first Tuesday of November. On 20 January 1981, he took the oath of the presidency of the most powerful nation in the world. From day one, he intensified the arms race with the Soviet Union and took the first steps to unite the world through the World Wide Web and Internet services, thus taking the world by storm. The Armed Forces of the United States were the first to get experimental use of the World Wide Web, and very quickly, the entire world was covered by a phenomenon called the Internet.

In the beginning, that is, during most of the 1980s, we had very rudimentary types of computers in the offices for basic work like typing letters, maintaining our internal departmental databases, and accomplishing accounting. As the research spearheaded by San Francisco-based firms advanced, our computers were replaced by better ones. Slowly and steadily, we were entering the phase of using the Google search engine. Electronic mail messaging started as well, thus reaching far-off destinations in seconds. Suddenly, we discovered that the world was one. America started sharing useful and useless information with the less privileged world.

The Soviet Union had a smaller economy than the United States, and during the race for armed supremacy, it could not keep pace with the much bigger fiscal reservoir of America. Financially exhausted by the unsustainable arms race with America, suddenly, the Soviet Union started collapsing bit by bit. The American economy got stressed, too, but even after taking serious falls and bumps, it carried on. Soon after, Facebook and YouTube came in, and social media became the new norm. As time passed, WhatsApp arrived, too, and the whole world got further 'united'. Most of the servers and storage of data facilities were in the United States. Both the Soviet Union and China started objecting to American hegemony, but the rest of the world trusted the United States to ensure the safe custody of their data. Now, some countries, like India and China, want to control the use of Internet storage and have access to the stored material. America is resisting this by citing reasons for privacy. The Internet storm has invaded the world, but common folks are enjoying it.

A 32-Year-Long Wait for ₹17,000

It was a cool Patiala autumn morning in 1979 when I arrived at my office of Executive Engineer Works in the Punjab Public Works Department (Buildings and Roads Branch) on the picturesque heritage structure on Mall Road. I noticed an infirm-looking, trembling man sitting on a vintage wooden bench outside my office. The peon opened the door for me, and I got in. The old guy kept sitting on the bench quietly, yawning and dozing off occasionally. After a couple of hours, I asked my peon to let him in. The peon told me that this man was in the habit of visiting the office every few months, that he had nothing else to do, and would keep bugging the officials. I told him to simply send him in; no ifs and buts.

The gentleman told me a 32-year-old story of Sargodha in the Rawalpindi division of West Punjab in his feeble voice in the Pothohari Punjabi dialect. He used to be a building contractor who built the boundary wall of a school in Sargodha. The work was finished well before August 1947. He applied for his final payment. His bill was in the process of payment when the creation of Pakistan was announced. Rather than getting his payment, he was forced to leave Pakistan, virtually penniless. He reached India, tired and battered. After a couple of years, things stabilised, and he visited Sargodha to claim his final payment. The Public Works Department of West Punjab authorities in Sargodha told him that in accordance with the mutually accepted arrangement, those Hindus and Sikhs who had worked in Pakistan and had migrated to India were to be paid in India, and those Muslims who had worked in India and had migrated to Pakistan, their claims were to be settled in Pakistan.

I cross-checked with the office veterans; his version was confirmed. However, when he applied for payment in India, he was told to produce the original records. He went back to Pakistan. The authorities there reluctantly promised to give him all the records, barring the original measurement book. In India, the authorities refused to pay him without verification from the actual measurement book. He went back to Pakistan, and contrary to the regulations, as a gesture of goodwill, the concerned overseer gave him the measurement book. He showed me the old, worn-out book. It confirmed the completion of the work and an outstanding payment of a little more than ₹17,000.

The old man expressed his desire to get this final payment before his death. I sent it to the concerned office superintendent. The office superintendent was initially hesitant to come, but when he turned up, he told me that the file was lost. I was flabbergasted. I called the record keeper; she was a young girl fresh from college and untainted by corruption. She informed me that the file was not lost and that it was in the drawer of the concerned office superintendent. I again sent for the superintendent; this time, he looked worried. He told me that he would produce the file before 5 p.m. I said that I wanted it immediately without any further delay. He could read my face and make out that I was serious. So, he brought the file to me complete with his and his assistant's favourable notings by 2 p.m. I meticulously went through the entire file, recorded my notings, and put it up for the orders of the chief engineer. There was no dearth of honest officers during those days. The chief engineer, Sardar Bikram Singh Grewal, who is in his nineties now, was one of such fiercely honest officers. He was busy in meetings in Chandigarh all day. He came back at around 4 p.m. I explained the entire case to him and put up the file for his orders. Since it was due to the negligence of the department, the inordinate delay was condoned, and the chief engineer ordered prompt payment.

Catches Win Matches

In 1968, I was selected by the Union Public Service Commission (UPSC) to serve on the faculty of PEC, Chandigarh. The day I joined duty, my Head of Department, Professor R. C. Sharma, an alumnus of Purdue University in the USA, finding me young and energetic, asked me, 'Are you interested in administering a sport?'

I said, 'Of course.'

I had seen Dinesh Khanna of Amritsar winning laurels for his alma mater—PEC. Dinesh had won the Panjab University Chandigarh singles badminton title. He also went on to become India's national title holder. Professor Sharma thought I would want to administer badminton. But as a student for the past few years, I had seen some promise in the PEC cricket team. Some of them had gone to prestigious schools and were consistently very good performers. There were two outstanding players in the PEC squad. One was Gurmeet Singh from Uttar Pradesh—he was a medium-pace bowler and a brisk scoring opener. The other was a slow-scoring opening batsman and a good spinner, Amrik Singh. I thought they could be groomed

into a good combination of opening batsmen and a mixed pair of bowlers.

I asked Professor Sharma if he was interested in achieving good results or wanted to have someone merely fill a vacancy.

He said, 'Of course, I want to get good results.'

To this, I replied, 'Then give me cricket.'

His answer was, 'Someone already is heading cricket.'

I was alright, being the second-in-command, and so he readily agreed to my proposal. I was not a cricket expert, but I had heard the saying 'catches win matches'. I took my responsibility seriously. I would be on the ground at 4 p.m. sharp every day, without fail, and give the cricketing boys intensive practice about long-distance throwing and catching, including direct throws on the stumps. The intensive net practice was my second priority. Our boys were made to make accurate direct hits at the stumps. All these tactics were basic tips for cricketers from a non-cricket-knowing lover of sports. Some of the most hardworking players were from not-so-well-off families but were highly committed, nevertheless. They demanded that one kilogram of milk be given every day to each member of the cricketing squad. The college had no such policy, but I remembered the saying, 'Where there is a will, there is a way'. The milk was made available to them by circumventing the rules.

When the Panjab University inter-college championship season came, in the fall and winter, our team easily triumphed over all the teams of the Chandigarh zone, which was emerging as a competitive region. Guru Nanak Dev University was not yet in existence. The strongest team of the Chandigarh region was the local team of DAV College, Chandigarh—a very well-balanced team. Surprisingly, we conquered them too! The semi-final line-up included the strongest contenders—Hindu College Amritsar, DAV College Jalandhar, and DAV College Amritsar—but it was our college, PEC, that became the Cinderella team, first-time semi-finalists from an engineering college. Surprisingly, we won our semi-final too. The final was between the mighty Hindu College and us, the minnows. Everyone expected a massacre of the innocents by a mighty outfit. In the crunch match, we took every catch, and our boys made accurate throws at the stumps to generate runouts, which seemed virtually impossible. Our batsmen and bowlers showed true engineering precision. They grabbed every possible chance and squandered nothing away. When the match ended, we were the Panjab University champions, who triumphed over every team, though unexpectedly. We proved the adage right—catches do win matches. Needless to say, the college was overjoyed at this victory.

An Early Lesson in Austerity

My father, S. Sochet Singh, was nominated by the Patiala and East Punjab States Union (PEPSU) to the Constituent Assembly of India in 1949. I was five years old then. In hindsight, if we compare present-day Delhi with the Delhi of those days, it was a much smaller and cleaner city with wide boulevards lined with ornamental and shady trees.

According to the Census of India, 1941, composite (old and new combined) Delhi was a city of a little more than 5.5 lakh population, much smaller than Punjab's capital, Lahore, which was the fifth largest city in India. Most British officers left India in 1947, but some left at leisure.

As the sprawling houses were being vacated, the eligible Indians occupied them. Compared to around 800 Members of Parliament (MPs) today, the members of the Constituent Assembly, then, were about 300. So, every lawmaker could get a sprawling house. My father was allotted 22 Queensway (Janpath). He had a British-made Raleigh bicycle. All he needed was to keep it clean and properly inflated. Rather than taking shortcuts, he used to take the scenic Queensway-India Gate-

Kingsway (Rajpath) route to the Parliament House. This area is being renovated under the Central Vista project now.

Back then, his bicycle was treated with as much respect as a luxury car. On some occasions, he was allowed to take his spouse and children to the Parliament House. On one such occasion, I observed that almost all members were going in Baby Austins, Baby Morrises, French Reynolds, and Volkswagens, while some were being driven in luxurious Studebakers, Hillmans, Chevrolets, Buicks, Oldsmobiles, and Plymouths. On the other hand, my father, most of the time, rode a bicycle! My ego felt a little jolted, but I controlled my feelings.

For a few days, I hesitated to ask the awkward question to my father. One day, I finally plucked up the courage and asked, 'Father, most members commute between home and the Parliament House in plush automobiles, and you ride a bicycle... Why so?' His answer surprised me. He said, 'India is a poor country where everyone cannot afford a car.' He went on to say that a lot of well-to-do people in Europe had no shame in riding a bicycle to work, even when they could afford a car.

He must have read my mind, though. I think he felt hurt. Hence, though he did not buy a car, soon thereafter, he bought a USA-manufactured Willys Jeep to travel to the villages, which were devoid of metalled roads during those early days of independence.[1]

---

1. Previously published in *The Tribune*.

Table of Abbreviations

ABC	Australian Broadcasting Corporation
AIR	All India Radio
AM	Amplitude Modulation
BBC	British Broadcasting Corporation
BEL	Bharat Electronic Limited
BEST	Bombay Electric Supply and Transport
CBS	Columbia Broadcasting System
DD	Doordarshan
FM	Frequency Modulation
GEC	General Electric Company
GE	General Electric
IT	Information Technology
LSB	Lower Side Band
PEC	Punjab Engineering College
PEPSU	Patiala and East Punjab States Union
RM	Radio Moscow
RP	Radio Peking
SLBC	Sri Lanka Broadcasting Corporation
SOS	Save Our Souls
TB	Tuberculosis
UHF	Ultra-High Frequency
USB	Upper Side Band
VCR	Video Cassette Recorder
VHF	Very High Frequency

More Titles From The Browser

Ekarat: Stories He Left Behind
ISBN: 978-93-92210-08-2

Mahroks: The Story of the Kambojas, Sikhs and Shaheeds
Jewan Deepak
ISBN: 978-93-5737-645-7

The Nightingale and Other Stories
Maniki Deep
ISBN: 978-81-94954-27-9

Techtopia: How Carbon Met Silicon and Humans Entered the AI Black Hole
Kunal Nandwani
ISBN: 978-93-92210-94-5

Sociopreneur: Zero to One
Kunal Nandwani
ISBN: 978-93-88150-11-8

Wilderness Is Us: Hiking, Thriving and Learning in the Great Outdoors
Vipul Negi
ISBN: 978-93-88150-07-1

Because Time Does Not Heal
Sahar Gharachorlou
ISBN: 978-93-92210-10-5

Twice Born
Sahar Gharachorlou
ISBN: 978-93-88150-12-5

Wall Paintings: The Vanishing Treasure
Ram Partap Verma
ISBN: 978-93-88150-15-6

Sketch by the author